THE SIMPLE STARTUP

A Beginner's Guide To Starting A Business

Student Workbook

Copyright © 2019 ChooseFI Media, Inc.

All rights reserved. No part of this publication may be reproduced, distributed, or transmitted in any form or by any means, including photocopying, recording, or other electronic or mechanical methods, without the prior written permission of the publisher, except in the case of brief quotations embodied in critical reviews and certain other noncommercial uses permitted by copyright law. For permission requests, write to the publisher, addressed "Attention: Permissions Coordinator," at the address below.

ISBN: 978-0-9600589-5-2 (Paperback)

Library of Congress Control Number: 2019953694

All content reflects our opinion at a given time and can change as time progresses. All information should be taken as an opinion and should not be misconstrued for professional or legal advice. The contents of this book are informational in nature and are not legal or tax advice, and the authors and publishers are not engaged in the provision of legal, tax, or any other advice.

Layout and Design by Giada Mannino.

Printed by ChooseFI Media, Inc. in the United States of America.

First printing edition 2020.

Choose FI Media, Inc.
P.O. Box 3982
Glen Allen, VA 23058

www.choosefi.com
www.thesimplestartup.com

CONTENTS

	INTRODUCTION	1
SECTION 1	GENERATING A BUSINESS IDEA	2
SECTION 2	TEAMWORK & WORKING WITH OTHERS	10
SECTION 3	BUSINESS SNAPSHOT	16
SECTION 4	MARKET RESEARCH	24
SECTION 5	THE BUSINESS PLAN	30
SECTION 6	PRODUCTION PROCESS	40
SECTION 7	MARKETING MIX	46
SECTION 8	MARKETING & SALES	50
SECTION 9	COST, PRICE, PROFIT	60
SECTION 10	FINANCING	70
SECTION 11	THE PITCH	82
SECTION 12	FINAL REVIEW	88
	APPENDICES	93

INTRODUCTION

Welcome to The Simple StartUp. In your hands is the roadmap to business creation, taking you from an idea to a successful startup. In this workbook, you will learn about the various aspects of starting and running a business. You'll move from the idea generation phase of coming up with a business concept (or 10!) to starting your business and everything in between.

This workbook is structured in a way that will take you from idea to operation, and it's recommended that you go in order from Sections 1-12. You may come across words that you are not familiar with, which is normal when you are learning about something new! Definitions of most of these words can be found in the glossary at the end of this workbook or using an internet search. You can choose to complete this workbook on your own, with friends, or in your classroom. Consider exploring ideas and information from other resources to complement this workbook. Visit www.TheSimpleStartUp.com to find ideas, resources, and stories of others who have created their own successful startup business.

A good business should be something that you are interested in and excited about doing. You don't have to come up with the next world-changing invention to be an entrepreneur and business owner. Anyone can be an entrepreneur, and like most things, the more we practice it, the better we become. Good luck with your business!

– Rob Phelan

SECTION 1
Generating a Business Idea

A business is simply an organization that makes products or performs services for others to buy. An entreprenuer is the person who starts and owns the business and who takes on the risk of starting it with the plan of making a profit. By starting this workbook, you are now an entrepreneur and soon to be business owner!

Here are some tips to help you get started.

1. **Could your hobbies become a business?**
   What do you like to do in your free time? Many people have hobbies and skills which could be turned into worthwhile and profitable businesses. Make a list of your interests and hobbies, then brainstorm with your friends, family, or group members about how any of these could be turned into a business.

   For example:
   - **Carpentry or Welding:** Construct items from wood or metal for sale.
   - **Cooking:** Sell baked goods, make meals for busy families, create cookbooks.
   - **Technology:** Make a website, run social media campaigns, create instructional videos for video games, etc.
   - **Writing/Photography:** Take headshots, produce calendars, write freelance newspaper articles, start a blog, etc.
   - **Art:** Create coloring books for young children, take pet portraits, print custom t-shirts, etc.
   - **Music:** Offer classes, workshops, or form your own band.

2. **Are there any needs you can fill or problems you can solve?**
   What causes you frustration on a daily basis? What do you hear people complain about? What takes a long time to do, but could be done faster? Are there items or services people say they want, but can't easily get? Look for people's daily frustrations and then figure out a way to solve them.

   - **School:** Does your school have an after school food option? Can you take over concessions for a sport? Does a peer tutoring system exist or an intramural sports league?
   - **Home:** Can you mow lawns, walk dogs, or babysit?
   - **Local Community:** Is there a scarcity of locally produced craft items, school spirit wear, or tourist gifts/information? Could your local community benefit from a simple phrasebook in Spanish to enable better communications? Is there a guidebook or website for tourists coming to the area?

3. **Can you improve upon what's already out there?**
   Many businesses are formed simply because they look at an existing business and think they can improve it. Look around! What kind of businesses exist in your area? Are they doing a good job or can you see a way they could be better? Copy what works and improve upon weaknesses. One small change, and you have a new business idea.

4. **Use what you already have.**
   Take a look around your home and see what you already have that could be used in starting a business. Do you have equipment or materials lying around that could be used in a business? Make sure you have permission to use something from home before taking it!

5. **Keep a narrow focus.**
   A big mistake new entrepreneurs make is they try to go too broad, too fast! If you are going to do something with crafts, limit yourself to a small range of items that you produce. For services, do something really well, rather than a wide variety of things poorly. Identify a small niche product/service that will meet customer needs.

6. **Piggyback on hot trends.**
   There is a story about a man, Sam Brannan, from the California Gold Rush of 1848. Instead of getting sucked into the craze of searching for gold, he decided to buy all the shovels and picks in the city. He resold them to all the prospectors that were coming to town. By looking at the market a little differently, he was able to come up with a very lucrative business idea. Look for the current trends in your school, friend group, community, social media, retail news, etc. and think about how you can piggyback on this trend instead of participating directly in it. For example, what's the latest and greatest electronic device at the moment? Can you sell accessories for that device that your target market would be interested in? Things like cases, chargers, and apps can be personalized for a smaller market, such as school spirit customers, and sold directly to them.

7. **What do people ask you for help with?**
   People often think they need to be a professional or have a certification to be an expert in something. This is far from true, though! All you need to be is a little more informed than the people around you. What can you learn more about, or what do you already know about, that is more than the average person? Do people ask you for help or advice with anything? If so, you are a perceived expert in that area. How can you turn that into a business? Can you play guitar, fix computers, beat all your friends in a particular video game, or write very neatly? Turn that into a business that can make money for you!

Coming Up With Business Ideas

When it comes to generating business ideas, most will find it difficult at first. This is something we get better at, the more we practice it. Many people find that after they go through the process of coming up with business ideas, they often start seeing more and more opportunities every day. Make sure you have a place to record business ideas, whether on paper or a digital device (See Appendix 1).

> "You don't have to be a creative genius, invent an amazing product, or become an expert to make money as an entrepreneur.
>
> Entrepreneurship is all about finding inefficiencies in the system and figuring out how to capitalize on them."
>
> **Cody Berman**
> Fly To FI & Co-founder
> of Arsenal Discs

SECTION 1

BUSINESS ACTIVITY 1
IDENTIFYING OPTIONS

What do you like to do in your free time? Try to list at least 5 activities.

1. _____
2. _____
3. _____
4. _____
5. _____
6. _____

What skills do you have? What do you know how to do a little better than the average person? What do people ask you for help with?

1.	2.	3.
4.	5.	6.
7.	8.	9.

What are some problems you see in your school or community? What are people complaining about?

1. _____
2. _____
3. _____
4. _____
5. _____
6. _____

Brainstorming

The goal of brainstorming is to come up with and record as many different and diverse ideas as possible. Crazy and fantastical ideas are positive during brainstorming, not negative. Aim for a high quantity of ideas during brainstorming. Don't focus on the quality of the ideas right now. There will be plenty of time later to dissect and analyze them. Nothing should be discounted at this point in the process. Use the tips from the beginning of the section to inspire as many different ideas as you can.

Effective brainstorming can be done on your own or as part of a group. At this point in the workbook, you may still be working on your own, or you may have selected team members already. Either way, the process is the same, and it can be a good idea to brainstorm ideas on your own first. Then, meet as a group to share what you came up with, followed by a second round of brainstorming. This can be really effective after allowing some inspiration from what the others have suggested to influence your ideas.

Rules for Effective Brainstorming

- Do a practice run to warm up your mind. For example, how many uses can you think of for a paper clip?
- Assign one person in your group (it's you if you're working on your own) to write down ALL of the ideas that are generated by the group. Don't screen ideas at this point. Just write them all down.
- The quantity of ideas is better than the quality of ideas.
- There's no limit to what the ideas can be about, and don't worry about how they could be done at this point.
- Take your time, and don't pressure yourself to come up with one super idea. Allot some time for as many ideas to come out as possible. Then, maybe take a break before coming back to the list and seeing if you can come up with any more. Creating a living document, such as a phone note or Google Document, can make it easier for ideas to be added by you or a group later on.

At the end of the brainstorming session:

- Go through the list.
- Classify which ideas may be possible and which ones are not possible to take further in the time you have.
- Rank ideas based on how excited you are about doing them. You should aim for a business idea that you are excited about and can be implemented pretty easily.
- Start to brainstorm the positives and negatives of each idea that you think you could take further.
- Choose one idea to try and develop further.

"Always work hard on something uncomfortably exciting."

Larry Page
Co-founder of Google

If you are struggling to come up with ideas, check out Appendix 1 for a sample list of business ideas.

SECTION 1

Example Brainstorm

In an initial brainstorm, Alan, Mary, and Doug have each recorded some ideas they think would make great businesses for their school business project. Each person listed business ideas stemming from things that interested them or they felt they were better at than the average person.

They then met as a team and tried to look at each other's ideas to see if there was something they all wanted to do and would make a good business. They came up with 4 ideas that they all agreed upon.

Finally, they placed their 4 ideas on an Idea Display Chart using sticky notes to see which one they were most excited about and felt would be easy to get started.

The idea which excited everyone the most and seemed easy to start for the group is what they chose to do. If this ends up not being viable, their fallback idea is to run school events.

Alan
- Lemonade Stand
- Coffee Delivery Service
- Local Pictures Calendar
- Social Media Manager
- Essay Proofreader

Doug
- Dog Walking
- Car Washes
- Holiday Gift Baskets
- Hand-made Greeting Cards
- School Store

Mary
- Website Design
- Paint Store Windows for Holidays
- Sell Water and Candy at School Sports Events
- Organize Student Basketball League
- Drone Photography Service

1. Sell greeting cards and calendars with local photographs.
2. Run a school snack store.
3. Run websites and social media for other school businesses or local businesses.
4. Run school events such as a sports league, school dance, or field trip.

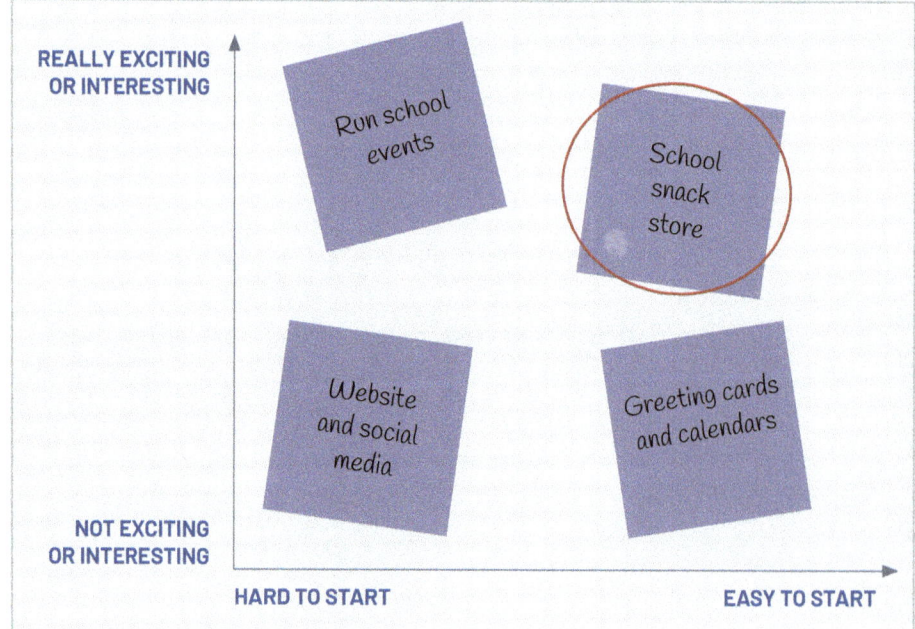

GENERATING A BUSINESS IDEA

BUSINESS ACTIVITY 2
POSSIBLE BUSINESS IDEAS

You can list as many ideas as you can think of, but start by trying to list 12 business ideas below.

1.	2.	3.	4.
5.	6.	7.	8.
9.	10.	11.	12.

The Idea Display Chart* below has 2 axes. The horizontal axis measures how easy an idea is to do from really difficult to really easy. The vertical axis measures how excited and passionate you are about an idea from not excited to really excited. For the ideas you've listed above, try placing each one on the chart (you can just write the idea number or the name of the idea).

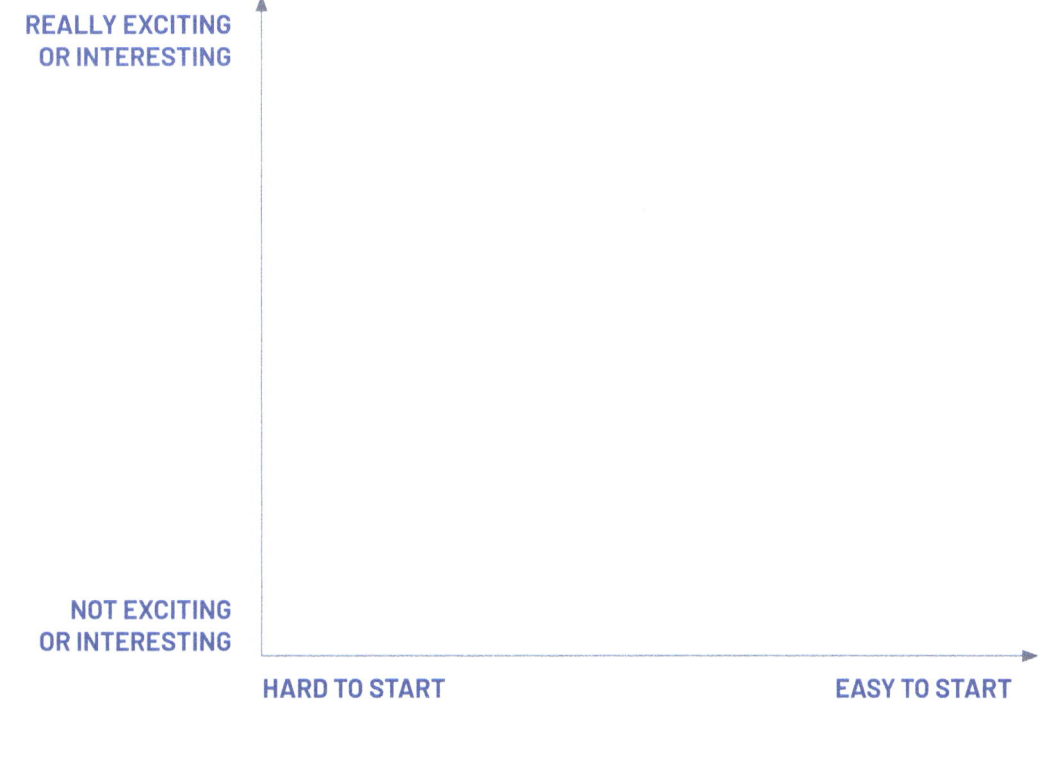

Which 3 ideas are you most passionate about and are easiest to start?

1. _____ 2. _____ 3. _____

*Adapted from Pop-up Business School (www.popupbusinessschool.co.uk)

SECTION 1

BUSINESS ACTIVITY 3
EVALUATING IDEAS

How did you come up with your different business ideas? Explain the process used.

How did you or your team evaluate the different ideas to figure out which ones to consider?

Which idea do you think is the strongest idea? Why?

How easy will it be to get your idea up and running as a business? Will it take a lot of time? What challenges do you foresee?

How excited and passionate are you (your team) about the business idea? Will you be able to stay motivated to keep working on it?

What did you learn through the process of generating ideas and then narrowing them down to one?

"Business can be a force for change. It can change and improve your life, those of your customers and the world around you. Entrepreneurship is how you change the world."

Alan Donegan
Co-founder, Pop-Up Business School

SECTION 2
Teamwork & Working With Others

Individual Business or Working with Others

Are you someone who typically likes to work alone, or do you thrive in being part of a team? Do you like to lead or prefer to follow? You will need to decide at this point which scenario you prefer. Working on your own means you get to have all the responsibility. You make all the decisions, do all the work, and get all the rewards. You are not reliant on anyone except yourself. A team brings different ideas and perspectives. You will be able to share the workload and let different team members work to their strengths. A team can help to keep the business moving by helping members to stay motivated and accountable.

Self-Analysis

When thinking about whether to do it alone, or be a part of a team, you must also consider yourself. Some people work really well on their own, and others need to be a part of a team to do their best work. Later in this section, we will look at business structure and how a team is set up. This can be a way to get people who like to work individually to function as part of a team. So don't write off a team just because you don't like working beside someone all the time.

Look at the following statements. Select if you agree or disagree with them. See if you can figure out whether you are better off on a team or working individually.

STATEMENT	AGREE	DISAGREE
When faced with a problem, I prefer to talk it through with others, rather than figure it out by myself.		
When something needs to get done (chores, homework, house projects) I need reminders from others or rewards to make sure they get done.		
Working with others gives me energy compared to working alone.		
I am able to delegate work and responsibilities to others and trust them to get it done.		
I don't have a lot of time to devote to all aspects of running a business.		

If you selected more "Agree" statements, you are probably best suited to working in a group. If you mostly "Disagree" with the statements, you might be better off working on your own.

What Skills Does Your Business Need?

What are your strengths and weaknesses? Do you possess the skills, determination, drive, and knowledge to accomplish your business idea on your own, or is being a part of a team going to help this business be successful? Effective businesses will have a blend of the following skills within their team.

Production Skills: What are the physical skills needed to be able to make the products or perform the services of your business? Do you need someone who is good with their hands and can build things? How about someone who is good with computers and can build spreadsheets, graphics, websites, etc.?

Organizational Skills: Are you really organized and good at keeping track of things that need to be done? Are you good at recording meeting notes and to-do lists, or tracking income and expenses? Can you make sure members of a team are doing their jobs and work is getting done?

Finance Skills: Do you have any experience with handling money for a business already? Are you able to make and maintain a budget for yourself? Do you like to make spreadsheets and make sure that all the numbers balance out for income and expenses? Do you have experience with using banks or digital payment systems?

Sales and Marketing Skills: These are very important skills, as someone in your business needs to be able to market the product or service and sell it. You will learn about these skills later in this workbook, but the more you have to start, the better. Do you have the social network and social media following that will allow you to promote your product to your target market? Do you have any connections in your network that will help you be successful? Are you a confident public speaker?

Remember you can always try to teach yourself any skills that you don't already have, but it may take time and you may not be as well-practiced as others are.

Pick Your Team

Now it's time to make a decision about working alone or working as part of a team. If you are going to work with others, make sure they are people who you know you can work with and who will do their share of the workload. Look for a diversity of skills, where others have some of the skills above that you don't possess yet or are weaker in. Some ways to build your team are:

- Advertise the skills/personality types you are looking for and see who responds.
- Target people that you know you want to work with and who will add to your business.
- Join with another individual or team who has a stronger business idea than yours, but you feel you can contribute to and help the business grow.

When the necessary skills have been identified, set ground rules for you and for the team.

- Agree who will take on responsibility for each of the different tasks.
- Decide how much time you are each prepared to invest in the business.
- Decide how you and the group propose settling problems/disagreements that may arise.

"Know what you bring. Know what you don't bring."

Angie Hicks
Co-founder of Angie's List

SECTION 2

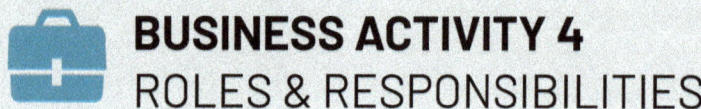
BUSINESS ACTIVITY 4
ROLES & RESPONSIBILITIES

In your business, there are lots of different roles and responsibilities that can be covered by one person, or split among a team. In the space below, list the team members for the business. Detail the strengths that each person might bring to the business and the roles and responsibilities of each member. Make sure to include production, organizational, finance, sales, and marketing skills that are needed to run your business.

TEAM MEMBER	STRENGTHS	ROLES & RESPONSIBILITIES

TEAM WORK & WORKING WITH OTHERS

Business Structure

Once you have settled on the members of the business, determined the roles and responsibilities of each member, and laid the ground rules for how the business will run, it can be helpful to visually display the members of the business and how they fit into the business structure. An organizational chart can be used to show the levels of the business and who reports to and communicates to each other.

Some businesses will delegate responsibilities based on skills and roles in the business, with everyone contributing to the same projects from within their role. Others will divide the running of the business into smaller projects and each member will be a leader of their project. They then direct the other team members when working on their project within the business. Some examples are below.

Try to think about the strengths, weaknesses, and personalities of the team members when choosing your structure. Does everyone want autonomy and control, or would they rather have one person be the leader, and they can simply complete their role and tasks given by the leader? If you are working on your own, you will have to fill every role and take on every responsibility.

"Coming together is a beginning, staying together is progress, and working together is success."

Henry Ford
Founder of Ford Motor Company

TOP DOWN FLOW CHART

- Managing Director
  - Marketing Manager
    - Social Media and Website Team
    - Social Media and Website Team
  - Finance Manager
    - Sales Team
    - Bank Liaison
  - Production Manager
    - Product A Team
    - Product B Team
  - Human Resource Manager

DIVISIONAL FLOW CHART

- Managing Director
  - Product A
  - Product B
  - Product C
  - Product D

SECTION 2

BUSINESS ACTIVITY 5
BUILDING A BUSINESS TEAM

Is your business being run by a single person or a team? How did you end up deciding on working solo vs a team?

What difficulties/concerns did you encounter in the process of deciding on your business team?

What did you learn about yourself in the process of self-analysis and team selection?

What are the skills that you or your team need to work on to be able to run the business effectively?

What does the organizational chart for your business look like? Sketch it in the space below. Include the roles and titles of members of the business.

TEAM WORK & WORKING WITH OTHERS

"Entrepreneurship might be one of the hardest things in the world to do, but your life is never boring."

Alex Fasulo
Freelance Writer and Professional Digital Nomad
www.alexfasulo.com

SECTION 3
Business Snapshot

Before you really get started in developing your business, it's important to try to identify what you think your business is going to look like. This is not a business plan! That will come later. This section will ask you to develop your ideas a little more to help give direction to you (and your partners) as you move forward with the business.

Business Snapshot

Completing a business snapshot at this point in your business development is going to really help to build a to-do list of action items needed to get your business started. You don't need to do any research at this stage, but rather put down on paper what you think your business is going to look like. When you envision your business up and running, what does it look like? As a team (or on your own), you will need to sit down and discuss each of the headings. Like the brainstorming done in Section 1, just write down thoughts and ideas. Later you can come back and evaluate those for their worth.

Business Synopsis: What does your business do? Why will it be a business that customers will want to use? What problem or need is your business trying to solve or accommodate?

Partnerships: Who are the other players that will help your business to run or be successful? This can include where you will buy your supplies from, who you will advertise with, who will sell your product, or mutually beneficial relationships between your business and others. What are each of these partners providing and do you know who/what businesses will fill those roles, and why?

Key Pieces: What are the things you need to do for your business to be successful? What are the steps you will take on a regular basis to run your business? These are things that make your Business Synopsis a reality.

Business Needs: What equipment, products, and services does your business need to get started and to operate on a daily basis? Examples could include: a table for sales, cashbox for money, plastic gloves if handling food, laptops for digital products and services, ingredients for food products, and materials for building crafts.

Customer Service: How important will customer service be to your business? Are you going to form relationships with customers, or will there just be a sale and that's it? Will you have any contact with your customer after the sale? How will you respond to questions or complaints? How easy will it be for customers to find information about the business, product, or service?

> Don't mimic others or try to follow a formula; that's not how you create something that's unique and therefore valuable. Instead, first clarify your ideas, then take action. That's how you'll create work that matters, which will allow your brand to stand out.
>
> Paula Pant
> Founder of Afford Anything

Target Market: Who is going to buy your product? How old are they? Where do they live/work? What job do they have? How much household income will they have? Do they have a particular hobby or interest?

Advertising: How are you going to let people know about your product and service? What media channels will you use?

Sales and Delivery: Where will the sale happen? Will it be in person or digitally? How will you get the product/service to them?

Business Costs: What do you think the costs will be to start and run your business? List them out and try to put a dollar amount to each one.

Business Pricing and Revenue: How is your business going to make money? How much do you think you are going to sell your products or services for? How many do you think you might sell in a week/month/year?

PARTNERSHIPS	KEY PIECES	BUSINESS SYNOPSIS	CUSTOMER SERVICE	TARGET MARKET
BUSINESS NEEDS			ADVERTISING	SALES & DELIVERY
BUSINESS COSTS			BUSINESS PRICING & REVENUE	

Adopted from the Business Canvas Model by Alexander Osterwalder (2005)

SECTION 3

> "A brand for a company is like a reputation for a person. You earn reputation by trying to do hard things well."
>
> Jeff Bezos
> Founder, CEO, and president of Amazon Inc.

Building Your Brand

Once you have a good idea of what your business is going to look like, start thinking about how you want to appear to the public. What is the image you want to portray and does it align with your business overview and values? Consider the following when building your brand.

What is your mission statement?

A mission statement describes how you intend to serve your target market. What do you want to accomplish and in what manner? Here are two example mission statements that highlight what the business is about:

- **IKEA:** To create a better everyday life for the many people.
- **Tesla:** To accelerate the world's transition to sustainable energy.

Your Business Name and Logo

You will need to create a business name and logo to convey the message you want to send about your business. A good name for a business should give the customer an indication of what the business does, for example "Kentucky Fried Chicken" or "Burger King". Of course, there are counter-examples to this. For instance, "Apple" does not provide any indication about what they do in their name. However, those businesses have to spend a lot of time and money informing their target market about their name and what they do. Your goal should be to avoid that and get your business going as cheaply as possible.

Your logo should follow the same line of thinking. Can you create something simple that either showcases the name of the business or includes a visual that displays what the business does? Like coming up with an idea for a business, you (and your team) should take some time to generate ideas for the business name and images for a logo. You can create free logos online using websites such as www.canva.com, or possibly look into drawing your own or finding a friend to design one for you.

Take a look at what a sample snapshot and logo might look like for a baking business, Sweet Treats.

BUSINESS SNAPSHOT

Sweet Treats

PARTNERSHIPS	KEY PIECES	BUSINESS SYNOPSIS	CUSTOMER SERVICE	TARGET MARKET
Costco (ingredients) School Principal Amazon (equipment and wrapping)	Get ingredients. Bake cookies and brownies. Wrap all goods. Sell on Tuesdays and Thursdays.	We are a company that sells cookies and brownies that taste really good, are gluten-free, and affordable for students. We will sell during lunch and after school when food isn't normally available.	Be really pleasant. Make sure all cookies and brownies are whole and replace broken ones.	Teachers and students in school. Town craft festival attendees.
BUSINESS NEEDS			**ADVERTISING**	**SALES & DELIVERY**
Aprons with logo Mixing bowls and pans Cash box Ingredients Wrapping for food items	Table Plastic gloves Napkins		School announcements School website Posters	Sell in school outside cafeteria. Take orders via text or in person. Pay with cash or Venmo.

BUSINESS COSTS	BUSINESS PRICING & REVENUE
Aprons with logo $30 Mixing bowls and pans $40 Ingredients $20 Wrapping for food items $5 Plastic Gloves $8 Total $103	Cookies $1 Brownies $1.50 Sell about 20 cookies and 10 brownies per day. Sell two days per week in school for 8 weeks, plus craft festival sales. Expected sales: about $700

SECTION 3

BUSINESS ACTIVITY 6
BUSINESS SNAPSHOT

Complete the business snapshot below.
Make sure you have considered all headings and the different facets of each.

PARTNERSHIPS	KEY PIECES	BUSINESS SYNOPSIS

BUSINESS NEEDS	

BUSINESS COSTS

20 | THE SIMPLE STARTUP

BUSINESS SNAPSHOT

CUSTOMER SERVICE	TARGET MARKET

ADVERTISING	SALES & DELIVERY

BUSINESS PRICING & REVENUE

Was there anything that came up during this exercise that causes concern for your business? Does it still seem like a good idea that can generate a profit?

STUDENT WORKBOOK

SECTION 3

BUSINESS ACTIVITY 7
BUILDING A BRAND

What does your business do? Write a brief description of the business.

What is the mission of your business? Write a brief mission statement.

Brainstorm business name ideas and jot down each name you consider. Even if a name seems unsuitable, you may end up using part of it when you narrow your list later. Choose a name that clearly reflects the industry you are in.

Choose a name that makes the industry you are in obvious. You don't want your potential customers having to guess what you're selling. If you are selling a craft, for example, you may do well to include the name of the craft in your business name. Write the name you want on paper and speak it aloud. This will help you determine whether you truly like the way it looks and sounds before you settle on it.

What is your Business Name: _____

Sketch some logo ideas in the spaces below or create and print digital logos which you can cut out and paste in the spaces. Circle the logo you are going to use for your business.

BUSINESS SNAPSHOT

"I have two pieces of advice for students. First, when forming your team, don't just go with your friends, instead try to link up with a group of students who have different skills that can benefit the business. Secondly, many students think that they have to charge a low price for a product/service just because they are students and feel that means it's not a "real" business. However, if you do the work on your market research and marketing mix, then you should be able to justify charging a premium price since you are meeting the needs of the market. Don't be afraid to charge what you're worth."

Alan Ryan
Founder of Déise College and Business Educator
at St. Augustine's College

SECTION 4
Market Research

A business is only a good idea if you have customers who want or need your product. Therefore, it's a good idea to find out what the wants and needs of the market are and how your business can best meet those needs. We call this process market research.

So what is market research and why do I need to do it?

At this point you've got an idea and you believe it's a good one. BUT, what if no one else thinks so? Conducting market research will give you valuable information about your future customers and will allow you to make informed decisions about how to set up your business to attract those customers. You want to make sure your product or service meets the wants and needs of the customer, so it makes sense to go find out what those are.

Where do you start?

1. Are there businesses, products, or services like yours out there already? What can you learn from them? What are they doing well? How could they be improved? How is your product/service going to be better than what is already available?

2. Go directly to your target customers: What are their needs? Use surveys, focus groups, and observation of behavior to determine what your potential customers want. You can also ask people with experience in the same industry as your idea. For example, if you are producing a craft, how about talking to a successful craftsperson in the area? They don't need to produce the exact same type of craft as you, but they are still trying to sell to a similar customer. Ask them for advice and help with getting started.

When giving a survey to your market, consider the two types of data you can collect:

Quantitative Data: measures of values or counts usually expressed as numbers. Example questions can include "How many? How much? or How often?"

Qualitative Data: measures of 'types' and may be represented by a name, symbol, or a number code. Examples can include questions such as "what is your favorite _____?": color, model car, food, etc.

"We think mistakenly, that success is the result of the amount of the time we put in at work, instead of the quality of the time we put in."

Arianna Huffington
Founder of The Huffington Post and Thrive Global

What are the different types of Market Research?

There are two main types of market research:

Primary/Field Research: involves gathering new data that has not been collected before. For example, observing behaviors, surveys, or interviews with groups of people in a focus group.

Secondary/Desk Research: involves gathering existing data that has already been produced. You can find this on blogs, websites, business reports, market trends, books, or newspapers. Things you might look for are competitors, pricing, market size, income levels, etc.

It is important that you carry out both types of research and to use the results of your research to determine if you have a viable business idea.

Define Your Target Market

Your target market consists of the make-up of the typical customer who is going to want to buy your product or service. Given the competitive nature of business, having a well-defined target market is more important than ever. No one can afford to target everyone and a common mistake of new businesses is to say "everyone" is the target market. Small businesses can effectively compete with larger businesses by targeting a niche market. This is where you have a very particular segment of the market that you are targeting to be your customers.

Many businesses say they target "anyone interested in my services." Some say they target small-business owners, students, homeowners, or stay-at-home parents. All of these targets are too general.

Some examples of a well-defined target market includes:

- Students at StartUp High School who stay after school for non-athletic events such as drama, tutoring, academic clubs, and honors societies. (Target for a after school snack store)
- StartUp High students in their junior year, who are not taking a Fall Semester Math or English class and who are interested in going to college. (Target market for a SAT prep tutoring service)

Targeting a specific market does not mean that you are excluding people who do not fit your criteria. Rather, target marketing allows you to focus your marketing budget and brand message on a specific market that is more likely to buy from you than other markets. This is a much more affordable, efficient, and effective way to reach potential customers and generate business.

Who do you think is going to want your product?

When you divide the population into smaller subgroups based on different characteristics, this is called market segmentation. When you imagine your

> "An entrepreneur is an innovator, a job creator, a game-changer, a business leader, a disruptor, an adventurer."
>
> **Sir Richard Branson**
> Founder of Virgin Group

customer, who are they? How old are they? Where do they live? How much money do they make? What are their interests? What level of education do they have? Are they single, married, or part of a family? What job do they have?

In defining your target market, you should be able to answer all of those questions with as much detail as possible. Some ways to help you develop this:

1. Who are your competitors and who is buying their product or service?
2. What are the benefits of your product? Who is likely to want those benefits?
3. Who already owns or uses the product or service that you want to provide?
4. How much are people currently paying for products or services similar to yours?

What are the main stages in carrying out market research?

1. Identify what you want to know about the market. When starting a business, you are concerned with answering:

    - Who is going to buy your product/service?
    - What do they want to buy?
    - Where do they want to buy it?
    - When do they want to buy?
    - Why they will want your product/service?
    - How much they are willing to pay for it?

2. What information is needed to answer these questions? Can you find it using existing sources or do you need to include it in your primary research?
3. Choose the method(s) to conduct your research. Will you use something like a survey or focus group? What websites may provide the information you need?
4. Carry out your research.
5. Analyze the results to answer your questions.
6. Make decisions about the business based on your market research.

MARKET RESEARCH

BUSINESS ACTIVITY 8
MARKET RESEARCH

Describe the primary (field) research you conducted for your business. If you conducted a survey* or focus group, include the questions you used.

_____
_____
_____
_____
_____

Describe the secondary (desk) research you conducted for your business. What sources did you use? What questions did you aim to answer?

_____
_____
_____
_____
_____

What are the results of your market research?

_____
_____
_____
_____

How will your results effect your business decisions moving forward? Do you need to make changes to your product/service?

_____
_____
_____
_____
_____

*Include a copy of the survey you gave with this activity and in your appendices of your business plan.

SECTION 4

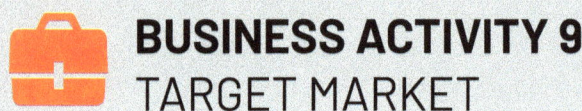
BUSINESS ACTIVITY 9
TARGET MARKET

Who is your target market? If one of the criteria doesn't apply to your product or service, just put "all."

Age: _____

Location: _____

Gender: _____

Income level: _____

Education level: _____

Marital or family status: _____

Occupation: _____

Ethnic background: _____

Personality: _____

Attitudes: _____

Values: _____

Interests/hobbies: _____

Lifestyles: _____

Behaviors: _____

Once you've decided on a target market, be sure to consider the following questions. (Write a short response to each)

How many people are there who fit my target market criteria? _____
_____

Will my target market really benefit from my product/service? Will they see a need for it? _____
_____

Do I understand what drives my target market to make decisions? _____
_____

Can they afford my product/service? _____
_____

Can I reach them with my message? Are they easily accessible? _____
_____

MARKET RESEARCH

"Launching products is easy—it's building it, finding the right manufacturers, getting the design right, and all of the marketing that is hard."

Jessica Alba
Cofounder of The Honest Company

SECTION 5
The Business Plan

S.W.O.T. ANALYSIS

After completing your market research, you're almost ready to start your business. The next step is to do a S.W.O.T. (Strength, Weaknesses, Opportunities, Threats) analysis of your business idea before moving any further towards starting the business.

What is a S.W.O.T. Analysis?

A S.W.O.T. analysis is used to let you know what potential problems you might encounter in your business and the things that will benefit your business. Carrying out a S.W.O.T. analysis involves looking at strengths, weaknesses, opportunities, and threats. Since you feel positive about your business, this analysis can be difficult to run on your own. It's important to approach this with an analytical mind and really consider all aspects of the business. It will help save you from potential failures and identify areas for possible future growth.

- Strengths and Weaknesses relate to internal factors (things within your business) over which you have some control.

- Opportunities and Threats relate to external factors (things outside your business) over which you have limited or no control.

> "Differentiate yourself! Why are you different? What's important about you? Why does the customer need you?"
>
> **Sara Blakely**
> Founder of Spanx

STRENGTHS	WEAKNESSES
■ Things your business does well ■ Qualities that set you apart from your competitors ■ Internal resources such as skills or knowledgeable staff ■ Tangible assets such as intellectual property, capital, technologies, etc.	■ Things that your business lacks ■ Things that your competitors do better than you ■ Resource limitations ■ Unclear unique selling point (USP)
OPPORTUNITIES	**THREATS**
■ A need in the market that is not currently being filled ■ Few competitors in the area ■ Emerging need for your product or service ■ Press/media coverage of your business ■ Large network to use	■ Emerging competitors ■ Changes in regulation/rules ■ Negative press ■ Changing customer habits (fads dying)

THE BUSINESS PLAN

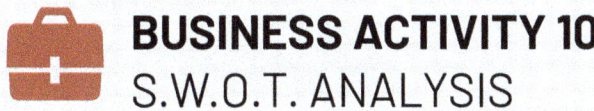

BUSINESS ACTIVITY 10
S.W.O.T. ANALYSIS

Conduct a S.W.O.T. analysis of your business

Identify the **STRENGTHS** of your business	Identify the **WEAKNESSES** of your business
1.	1.
2.	2.
3.	3.
4.	4.

Identify the **OPPORTUNITIES** for your business	Identify the **THREATS** to your business
1.	1.
2.	2.
3.	3.
4.	4.

SECTION 5

Business Plan

A standard business plan consists of a single document divided into several sections including a description of: the organization, the market research, competitive analysis, sales strategies, capital and material requirements, and financial data.

The document can serve as the blueprint for your business. It helps business owners to consider all important aspects of their business and can be supplied to financial institutions or investors if financing is needed to get your business off the ground. You may also use your business plan if competing in a school or local competition, to give evaluators a concise yet detailed breakdown of your business.

A good business plan can help you get your thoughts organized. It can provide a guideline so you're not stuck looking at a blank page trying to figure out where to start. It also forces you to think about all aspects of the business and develop your idea into a viable business that can be successful. Alternatively, it can help you see that a business is not a good idea, which can save you a lot of hassle, heartache, and money!

You can choose to complete the business plan now and adapt it as you go through the rest of the workbook. Alternatively, it could also be written after you have gone through the other sections of the workbook and your business has been in operation for a short period. It's completely up to you! A business plan should always be a living document where you make changes and updates to it on a regular basis as you learn more about your business. The Business Activities of this workbook will help you in writing most of your plan.

> "Entrepreneurship has greatly changed my life. I was able to reach financial freedom, be my own boss, enjoy waking up everyday and working on my business, travel full-time, and more. My top advice for those interested in entrepreneurship is to start a business that you care about. Starting your own business will most likely take a lot of your time, so having it be something that allows you to pursue your passion either in work or in your free time is very important."
>
> **Michelle Schroeder-Gardner**
> Founder of Making Sense of Cents

Sections of a Business Plan

Title Page

Enter your business information including the business name, address, etc. If you already have a business logo, you can add it to the top or bottom of the title page.

Business Plan for "Business Name"

"Date"

"Business address"

"Phone"   Logo

"Email"

"Website"

Table of Contents:

Executive Summary ....Page #

Business Overview ....Page #

Market Analysis and Competition ....Page #

Sales and Marketing Plan ....Page #

Ownership and Management Plan ....Page #

Operating Plan ....Page #

Financial Plan ....Page #

Appendices ....Page #

Section 1: Executive Summary

The executive summary goes at the beginning of the plan, but is written last. It provides a short, concise, and optimistic overview of your business that captures the reader's attention and creates a need to learn more. The executive summary should be no more than two pages long, with brief summaries of other sections of the plan.

- Describe your mission - what is the need for your new business and what do you hope to accomplish?
- Introduce your business, the management, and ownership.
- Describe your main product and service offerings.
- Describe the customer base you will be targeting and how your business will serve those customers.
- Summarize the competition and how you will get market share (what is your competitive advantage?).
- Briefly outline your financial projections for the first few years of operation.
- Describe your start-up financing requirements (if applicable).
- An overview of the industry and how your business will compete in the sector.

Section 2: Business Overview

Describes the overall nature of the business. What industry are you in?

- Are you in the food, technology, hospitality, automotive, telecommunications, etc. industry?
- Describe your business and how it fits into that industry.
- Describe the existing competition in your industry. Give highlights of who your main competitors are.
- Describe what your unique selling point is (new, improved, lower cost services, etc.).
- The S.W.O.T. Analysis of your business. (Business Activity 10)

Section 3: Market Analysis and the Competition

In this section, you need to demonstrate that you have thoroughly analyzed the target market and that there is enough demand for your product or service to make your business viable. Refer to your primary and secondary market research. In this section you should include a detailed assessment of your competition and how your business will compete in the sector.

- Define the target market(s) for your product or service in your geographic locale. (Business Activity 9)
- Describe the need for your products or services.
- Estimate the overall size of the market and the units of your product or service the target market might buy, potential repeat purchase volume, and how the market might be affected by economic or demographic changes.
- Estimate the volume and value of your sales in comparison with any existing competitors.

- Explain any reasons why it will not be easy for others to replicate your business or take your customers.
- Describe your direct competition and indirect competition for sales.

Section 4: Sales and Marketing Plan

A sales and marketing plan is a description of how you intend to entice customers to buy your product(s) or service(s). We refer to this as the marketing mix of a business. It consists of the 5 P's: Product, Price, Promotion, Place, and Packaging. This will be covered in further detail in later sections of this workbook, but you can consider each of the sections now, and then come back and edit it after learning more and completing Business Activity 15. A business plan can, and should be, a living document. Always available to change and update as you learn more!

- **Product** - Describe your product or service, how it benefits the customer, and what sets it apart from competitor offerings. What is your Unique Selling Point (USP)?
- **Price** - Describe how you intend to price your product or service. Pricing has to be competitive to attract customers, but high enough to cover costs and generate a profit. Pricing can be based on a markup from the cost to produce, value to the buyer, or in comparison with similar products/services in the marketplace. Include your break-even analysis too. (Business Activity 19, 20)
- **Promotion** - List the different media you will use to get your message to customers (e.g. business website, email, social media, traditional media like newspapers, flyers, banners, signs, etc.). Will you use sales promotional methods such as free samples, product demonstrations, etc.? (Business Activity 16,17,18)
- **Place** - Describe how you will distribute your products to the customer or where you will be providing the services. How will your customers find you?
- **Packaging** - What type of packaging will be required? How will the product(s) be shipped? Will the product be aesthetically pleasing to look at or presented in such a way that is appealing? For example, a gift basket that isn't dressed up and made to look appealing does not serve its true purpose.
- **Another thing to consider:** What methods will be used for payment? Cash, checks, cards, digital?

THE BUSINESS PLAN

Section 5: Ownership and Management Plan

This section describes the legal, ownership, and management structure, as well as staffing requirements of your business.

- **Ownership Structure** - Describe the legal structure of your business: corporation, partnership, Limited Liability Business, or sole proprietorship. List ownership percentages if applicable. As you start your business, you will most likely be working as a sole proprietorship or partnership, but should you wish to explore creating a business entity that is separate from your own, research how to set up a LLC or consult with an accountant.

- **Management Team** - Describe the roles of the members of the business. Is there a hierarchy to the business structure? What is each person responsible for? (Business Activity 4,5)

- **Human Resources** - List the type and number of employees or contractors you will need and an estimate of the cost and financial benefit of each. How much you are paying them and what extra revenue they bring to the business as a result of having them?

- **External Resources and Services** - List any external professional resources required, such as graphic designers, trades people, accountants, lawyers, consultants, etc.

Section 6: Operating Plan

The operating plan outlines the physical requirements of your business, such as a sales table, storage, retail space, equipment, inventory and supplies, labor, etc. For a one-person, home-based digital business the operating plan will be short and simple, but for a business such as a food supplier or craft manufacturer that requires custom facilities, specialized equipment, and multiple staff members, the operating plan needs to be more detailed.

- **Location or Potential Locations** - Explain what you have done to date in terms of identifying possible locations, sources of equipment, supply chains, etc. Do you need to get permission or pay rent to anyone?

- **Production** - Explain how long it takes to produce a unit of your product or provide one unit of service. If you haven't started already, identify when you'll be able to start producing your product or service. Include factors that may affect the time frame of production and how you'll deal with potential problems such as rush orders.
(Business Activity 13,14)

- **Staffing** - Outline expected staffing needs and the main duties of staff members, especially the key employees. Describe how the employees will be sourced and the employment relationship (contract, full-time, part-time, etc.). Detail employee training needed and how it will be provided.

- **Equipment** - Include a list of any equipment needed. Include the cost and whether it will be leased, borrowed, or purchased, and the sources. (Business Activity 14)

- **Supplies** - If your business is in manufacturing, retail, food services, etc. include a description of the materials needed and how you will reliably source them. Give descriptions of major suppliers if needed. Describe how you will manage inventory. (Business Activity 14)

Section 7: Financial Plan

The financial plan section is arguably the most important section of the business plan. Even though the goal of your business should be to start for little to no money, the financial plan is important if you need to borrow money or want to attract investors. The financial plan has to demonstrate that your business will grow and be profitable. To do this, you will need to create projected cashflow forecasts, cashflow statements, and balance sheets. (Business Activity 22,23,24,25) For a new business, these are forecasts. A good rule of thumb is to underestimate revenues and overestimate expenses. This section will also be covered in further detail later in this workbook.

Include the following financial statements:

- **Cashflow Forecast** - Shows your anticipated cash revenues and expenses on a regular time increment (weekly or monthly). It is important for demonstrating that you can manage your cashflow and will be a good investment.

- **Cashflow Statements** - Shows your actual revenues, expenses, and profit. Do this on a monthly basis for at least the first year for a startup business.

- **Balance Sheet** - A snapshot summary of the assets, liabilities, and equity of your business at a particular point in time. For a startup, this would be on the day the business opens. This is comparable to the net worth calculation of an individual.

- **Break-even Analysis** - Will demonstrate to loan providers or investors what level of sales you need to achieve to make a profit. Add in charts to visually demonstrate. (Business Activity 21)

Section 8: Appendices

The appendices and exhibits section contains any detailed information needed to support other sections of the plan.

Possible Appendix Items:

- Detailed market research and analysis of competitors such as copies of surveys and results, transcripts of interviews, notes from observations, etc.
- Resumés of the owners and key employees
- Additional information about your industry
- Additional information about your products/services
- Site/building/office plans
- Copies of mortgage documents, equipment leases, etc. (or quotes on these)
- Marketing brochures and other materials
- References from business colleagues
- Links to your business social media accounts and screenshots of homepages
- Any other supporting material that may impress potential lenders or investors if you are looking for financing
- Credit histories for the business owners

See Appendix 4 for an example business plan for Sweet Treats

THE BUSINESS PLAN

BUSINESS ACTIVITY 11
BUSINESS PLAN: BUSINESS OVERVIEW

The business overview describes the overall nature of the business. It lets the reader know what industry the business is going to be in (food, crafts, landscaping, auto, tech, travel, education, etc.) and how it will fit into that industry. Try to complete one now, and then again later after you have been in operation for some time.

What industry are you in? What are the trends of this industry? Is it a new or established industry? How has it developed in the area?

Describe your business and how it fits into the industry.

Describe the existing competition in the industry.

What is your USP? What sets you apart from the competition? (new, improved, lower cost services, etc.)

STUDENT WORKBOOK | 37

SECTION 5

 # BUSINESS ACTIVITY 12
BUSINESS PLAN: THE MARKET & THE COMPETITION

At this point you've identified who your target market is and some of their preferences towards your product. The question is, though, is there going to be enough customer spending to go around and accommodate your business in the market?

Describe the need for your product or service. What makes you believe that your product or service will sell? Make reference to your market research in your answer.

_____
_____
_____
_____
_____
_____
_____
_____

Estimate the size of the market and how many units of your product or service you estimate each person will buy. What are your numbers based on? Include reference to your market research.

_____
_____
_____
_____

How much money does your target market currently spend with your competitors? Try to estimate as close as possible. How will you compare to your competitors when you start your business?

_____
_____
_____
_____

THE BUSINESS PLAN

"You don't have to graduate from an Ivy League school, and work at a particular place, and get an MBA to start a billion-dollar company. But you have to have a purpose. If you start a company because you think you should, but your heart is not in it that won't give you the fuel to get through the hard stuff. We had the passion, so when challenges happened, we knew how to push through it."

Jen Rubio
Co-founder, President, and Chief Brand Officer of Away

SECTION 6
Production Process

"Your most unhappy customers are your greatest source of learning."

Bill Gates
Founder of Microsoft

When considering the core of your business, it is essential to identify all of the parts that go into delivering your product or service. Expect this to be a practice of trial and error before you settle on a process that is best for your business. You may need to change some of the materials you use, or where you source them from if difficulties or inefficiencies arise. With a service, it is essential to verify that all elements can be delivered, to the desired standard, within the allocated budget. Failure to complete this stage can mean costs being unnecessarily high, or profits disappearing due to disruptions in the process.

Your previous market research should have given you a clear indication of the types of products/services that are in demand in the marketplace. Customer preferences change and these changes are generally reflected in social media, local media, and advertising. Make sure you are paying attention and checking your market on a regular basis to keep up with their needs and wants.

A common misconception is that an entrepreneur should produce all goods or perform all services themselves. In fact, a good business will look to outsource or subcontract parts of the business that:

- **Take up a large amount of time or can be done faster by someone else.** An example of this would be hiring someone to make a basic website for you in much less time than you can. This will allow you to use your time more productively in other aspects of the business.

- **Requires a higher level of skill than the team possesses.** An example would be a business that wants to sell hand painted bird houses. The business owners may have the skills to paint at a high level but they choose to hire someone else to build the bird houses or buy them pre-made.

- **Needs qualifications or specializations that do not exist within the team.** A business looking to flip cars (buy a car, fix it, then sell it for a higher price) might need to hire a mechanic to do the repairs on a car before they try to sell it.

- **Are high cost to do in small quantities.** A t-shirt printing business could buy their own heat press machine, t-shirts, and color screen printer for producing shirts for their business, but the cost of all that equipment would be part of their costs in producing the shirts. Instead they submit their designs to a large scale printing service and that company produces the shirts for much cheaper due to the high volume of shirts they print.

- **Can be carried out by someone else which allows energy to be spent elsewhere in the business.** A food delivery business decides to hire someone else to drive and pickup food while they concentrate on developing their website and finding new customers. Driving a car is a skill that most people could do, but the website and sales side of the business need the owner's attention.

Minimum Viable Product

When it comes to finally selling to the public, many entrepreneurs get stuck in a state of paralysis as they keep trying to improve their product and conduct more market research, before actually approaching someone for a sale. A minimum viable product (MVP) approach means you will go to the customers as early as possible, try to sell your product in its early stage, and then make changes based on customer feedback. This may mean going through the Development Process on the next page several times before you feel you have "got it right".

Your MVP should be your business idea at its most basic. Don't spend a lot of time adding on extra features or trying to make it look really cool. Get your business in front of customers as early as possible and then start making changes or additions based on their feedback.

An example of this is a startup business that had the idea to develop an app for students to connect with tutors in their school if they needed help with homework. They knew there was a demand for a tutoring service from their market research and felt building an app was the best way to facilitate that. They planned to include an appointment booking system and a payment system as exciting additional features. Before they moved forward with building the app, they determined that they should start with an MVP. For them, this meant creating a simple document with a couple of the names of the prospective tutors, their area of expertise, and a contact number for them. They displayed the document around the school and then asked students what their feedback was after a week. As it turned out, their simple method was very successful because the poster around the school was a great reminder for students to set up tutoring and they preferred to communicate directly with the tutor. Additional feedback was that parents also wanted access to the tutor list. Instead of taking weeks to create a feature packed app, they were able to charge tutors each week to display their names on their poster and they also emailed home a copy of the tutor list to parents. Their business got up and running very quickly and shortly afterwards, they made a basic webpage with tutors listed and a space for students to leave reviews of their tutors.

Production Estimation

A well-organized production system is necessary to ensure that orders can be delivered on time. You need to ensure that if you make a sale, you have the ability and resources to provide the product or service to the customer, in the time agreed. Be mindful of how much material you buy. There is a risk that too much or too little materials may be purchased. Too little and you lose potential sales. Too much and you end up having a lot of your business's money tied up in materials that can't be sold. It is advisable to take advance orders with a deposit in order to gauge the quantities required and reduce the initial capital needed to start.

> "Successful entrepreneurs do not give up at the first sign of trouble, nor do they persevere the plane right into the ground. Instead, they possess a unique combination of perseverance and flexibility."
>
> **Eric Ries**
> Author of The Lean StartUp

Quality Control

Quality control is essential in all businesses to ensure that customers are satisfied. Quality control is the system you put in place to make sure all products and services meet the minimum required standards of your business. Create a checklist or test to check all units against to ensure your quality stays at the desired level. It's recommended to appoint someone in the business team with responsibility for overseeing production and quality.

Quality control can include headings such as: appearance, function, performance, size, packaging, defects, taste, etc. As a team (or on your own), decide what standards are important to have in your product or service, and at what point is it unsuitable for customers to use/receive.

The Development Process

If you are planning on offering a product or service, it is important to first go through the development process before increasing production or marketing.

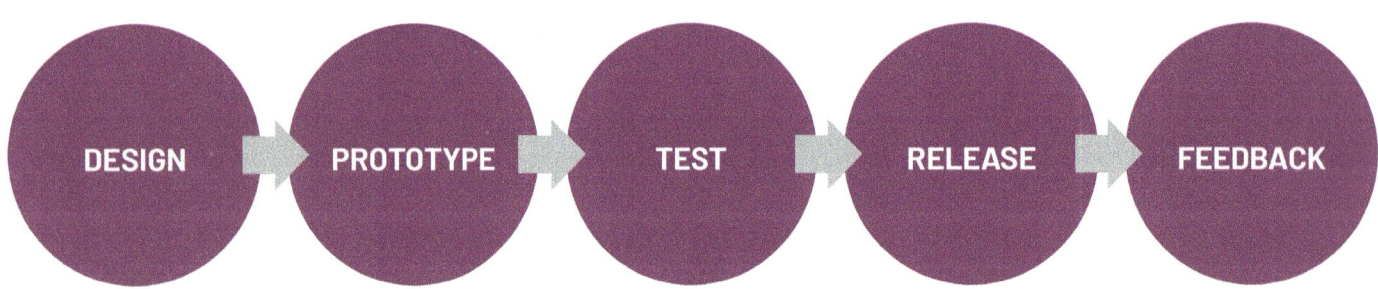

Design

Sketch it out or write down what the product/service will: do, look like, be made of, operate like, or be assembled by. This is the blueprint of what will make the product or service a reality.

Prototype

Create a small working model of your product. This will allow you to work out any issues in how you make the product before producing in larger quantities. For services, doing small test runs or trials with family/friends is a great way to figure out your processes and what might need to change before nailing down your final offering. Figure out how long it takes you to make a unit or perform a single service. It is reasonable to predict that you will get faster as you practice more.

Test

The last thing you want is to produce a product for a loss or sell a service for too high of a price because you didn't test it out first. Make a small quantity of your product and get it in the hands of your target market to see what they think. Do a small number of services in a place that is outside your target market in case you make mistakes or need to do some big changes. Look to get feedback from your customers. Does it function as described? Is it to the quality level that was expected? How long did it take to make or do? Is there anything that should be changed?

From here, you can go back to the design phase and make changes, or if you are satisfied with your product/service, move on to the big release!

Release

Now you can start producing in larger quantities and increase your advertising (Section 7 and 8). This doesn't necessarily end the production process. More often than not, you will have requests and recommendations from your customers. Any good business owner wants their customers to be completely happy with their purchase, and will look to make changes when needed.

Feedback

Always listen to what your customers are saying. The phrase "the customer is always right" rings true. If the customer doesn't like it, why should they buy it? Adjust, improve, and keep repeating the production process with your business.

SECTION 6

BUSINESS ACTIVITY 13
THE DEVELOPMENT PROCESS

Where will you (your team) produce the goods/provide the services for your business?

Who will produce the goods/provide the service?

How exactly will the goods be produced or the service rendered? What steps are involved?

What are some of the minimum standards you will expect to see in your product or service for it to be deemed high enough quality to be sold to your customers? How will you check for those standards?

What way will tasks/jobs be organized?

How long will it take to make the goods/provide the service?

BUSINESS ACTIVITY 14
PRODUCTION REVIEW

What steps in the Development Process have you already done? What did you learn?

Why are you doing it that way? What are the pros/cons about the method you have chosen?

What difficulties did you encounter or do you expect to encounter in the production process?

What did you learn in the process?

What equipment and materials will you need to produce your product or perform your service?

What feedback have you received from your market so far about your products/services?

SECTION 7
Marketing Mix

What is Marketing?

A market is the segment of the population who are potential buyers of your products or services. Your target market is the smaller subgroup who you believe are most likely to purchase from you. Marketing is the act of how you set up your business to meet the needs of your target market, and how you make your business as appealing as possible to that market in efforts to get them to buy from you.

The Marketing Process

You've already completed some of the initial steps for marketing in the previous sections of this workbook, and now you will take what you've learned from that and apply it to all aspects of how you set up and run your business.

Things you've already thought about or completed:

1. Identify a target market and what need, want, or problem area you are aiming to fill.
2. Conduct research on your target market to learn about their preferences and behaviors towards making purchasing decisions related to your business's products/services.
3. Begin to develop a brand and image for how you want the market to perceive your business and what you provide.
4. Finalize the products or services you are going to provide, and the process for making those happen that aligns with your business's brand.

Next up is the **marketing mix**. This is when you go deeper into the details of how your business is going to run now that you've done most of the preparation work. You are at the point where you can really start to think about when you want to begin selling to the public and turning your refined idea into a true business.

The next steps of the marketing process include:

5. Determine the price of your product or service.
6. Advertise and promote your business to your target market.
7. Start making sales.
8. Review, evaluate what is working and not working, and make changes as needed to continue to improve your business.

> "I'm convinced that about half of what separates successful entrepreneurs from the non-successful ones is pure perseverance."
>
> **Steve Jobs**
> Founder of Apple Inc.

The Marketing Mix

The marketing mix is one of the most well known phrases in the business world, yet it has different interpretations and meanings to each individual business. It will be up to you to take the elements discussed here and apply them to your unique business in the best way possible. The elements are the marketing 'tactics'. We will refer to them as the **'five Ps'** of the marketing mix. These elements are: **product**, **price**, **promotion**, **place**, and **packaging**.

When planning for the different aspects of your business, you need to view all decisions through the lens of what the customer wants or will buy. The question should always be "how do we adjust this aspect of the marketing mix to be the most appealing to our target market?"

"The way to get started is to quit talking and begin doing."

Walt Disney
Cofounder of The Walt Disney Company

Product

Use your market research to figure out what is important to the customer when they make buying decisions. Does your target market value the quality of a product, safety features, being environmentally friendly, or using local ingredients? Are you going to be a business concerned with Environment, Social, or Governance (ESG) issues? Is this going to be part of your unique selling point? Do you intend to provide any customer support after a sale has occurred?

Price

There's two major concerns when it comes to price: How much does the product/service cost to produce from beginning to final sale, and then how much is the customer willing to pay for it? There will be further thought put into determining the cost and price of your product later in this workbook. For now, find out what your competitors are charging. Do you have a unique product/service which you can charge more because no one else is competing directly with you?

Customers are constantly making value decisions when deciding on a purchase. Is the cost higher or lower than their valuation of the product or service? You will need to use your market research to determine what the market values your product/service at in order to answer this question. You can also decide to offer discounts or have special offers from time to time (for example: buying in large quantities or offering student discounts). You may have to adjust your pricing several times to find the "sweet spot" where you are maximizing profits.

Promotion

How will you draw attention to your business? Will you create posters, run a competition in your school or local paper, or utilize social media? Consider where your target market is located at different points in the day and how you can reach them during that time. What type of media does your target market consume? If you are selling a product, get a prototype or sample in the hands of your target market and compare your product to competitors. How will you present yourself if providing a service? Will you have a staff uniform or branded materials? Will you create a website or have business cards with key information about your business? Aim to keep costs as low as possible initially and use your network to find free or low cost opportunities to promote your business.

Place

You may have heard the popular phrase: "Location, location, location". Where you sell matters. This involves how easily you can get your product or service to the customer or for them to find you. Make it easy for your customers to buy from you. What type of places will you sell your products in? Will you only operate in your school/community or will you venture out to larger markets? Do you have access to transport? Will you make deliveries? Are you going to sell in person, face-to-face, or use other methods? This could include direct selling by mail order or internet sales using sites such as Etsy, Shopify, eBay, Facebook Marketplace, Amazon, etc.

Packaging

Packaging is a big part of the image you portray to customers. An area where many businesses fail is they don't consider how they are packaging their product or the way in which they present their service. Consider the appearance of your packaging, the color you choose, the image or logo which is your identity. It can say a lot about your business. Your customers may make a decision to buy from you based on eye-catching designs on your packaging. Service industries such as Uber and Airbnb have found that the same car or room, but with a few additional touches such as scent, decoration, personalized messages, and additional convenience products can have outsized returns in terms of feedback and the amount people are willing to pay for the service.

BUSINESS ACTIVITY 15
MARKETING MIX

What are some changes you will be making to your original product or service idea to meet the needs of your target market better?

How much do you think customers would be willing to pay for your product or service? What are you basing this answer on?

What type of advertising works for your product/service?

List all ways you will promote your business.

List some locations (physical and/or digital) where you can sell your product/service?

What considerations are you putting into the packaging of your product or additional touches for your service?

SECTION 8
Marketing & Sales

> "Successfully starting, building, and growing a business requires an owner to be confident and be able to demonstrate that confidence to employees, partners, customers, etc. Experience builds confidence, but knowledge through learning, reading, and listening was my biggest help. Learning never stops. We all teach, we all learn. For life!"
>
> **John Fitzgerald**
> Founder of Secure Code Warrior and SANS Securing The Human

Marketing vs Sales

As discussed in the previous section, marketing is the strategy you use to get your product or service in front of people, raise awareness, and build your brand. Sales is what you do afterwards. This is when you try to complete the deal and get the customer to commit to a purchase or engage a service.

The marketing phase aims to get customers to notice your product or service, explore your website or store, ask more questions or inquire about more information. Using the 5 P's of the marketing mix, you will need to develop a strategy for getting your target market into a position where sales can take over and you close the deal.

A popular marketing model is called the AIDA (**A**ttention, **I**nterest, **D**esire and **A**ction) model*, also known as the marketing funnel. This model describes the process that a potential customer will go through from being unaware of your business, all the way to the point where they make a purchase or engage your services. The metaphor of a funnel is used to visualize the number of people captured at each stage. In the beginning you are targeting your entire target market, and by the end you have a much reduced number of customers who decide to actually buy your product.

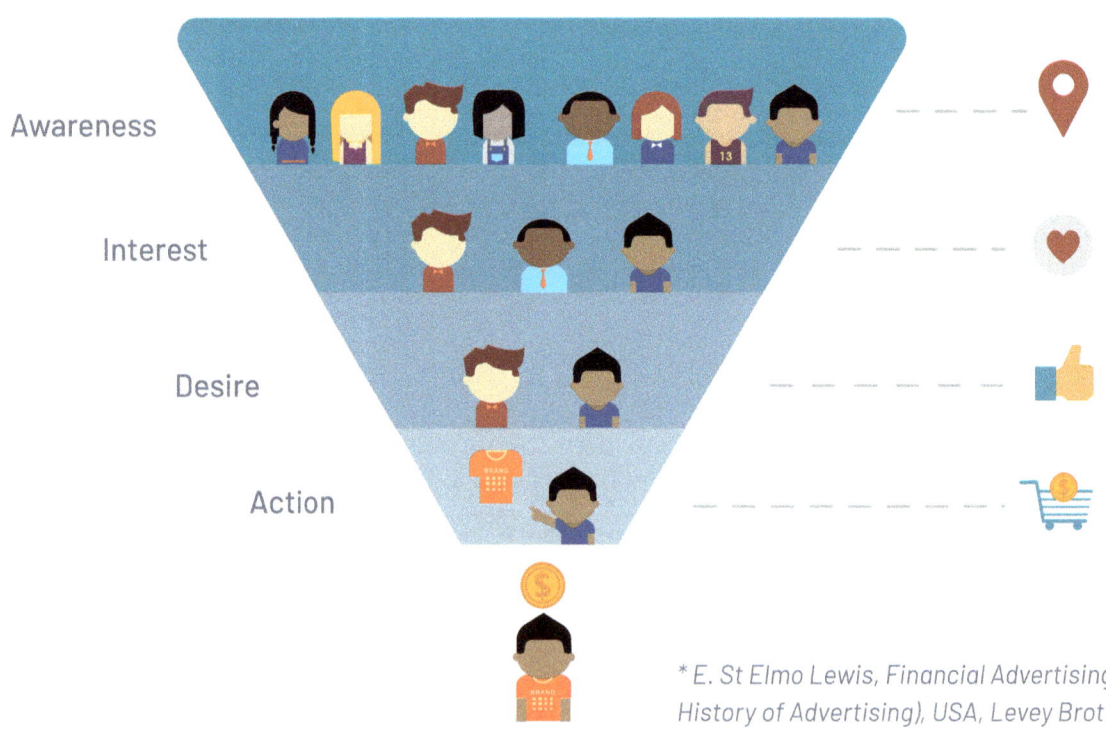

*E. St Elmo Lewis, Financial Advertising. (The History of Advertising), USA, Levey Brothers, 1908

50 | THE SIMPLE STARTUP

Awareness

All aspects of your marketing mix should be aimed towards your target market. Your marketing strategy starts with an advertising campaign. This is the plan of action for how you are going to get your message out to the customer. When deciding on your advertising campaign you will need to consider the following things:

1. **Advertising Budget** — How much are you willing to spend on advertising? Can you do it for free or very cheap through digital efforts, utilizing your network, and putting in time from the team? The more you can do yourself, the less you have to pay someone else to do!

2. **Media Channel** — What is the right type of media to use? It needs to reach your target market in the most effective and affordable way possible. Is it printed media such as letters, newspapers, magazines, flyers, posters, billboards? How about broadcast media such as school announcements, local radio, podcasts, or TV? Then there is the digital media market with options such as social media platforms, Google advertising, website advertisements, email, and texting. Or do you plan on using direct advertising strategies such as going door to door or cold calling potential customers?

3. **Selling Points** — What selling points are you going to emphasize to your target market? This should include, but not be limited to, your USP. Are you going to promote the uniqueness, functionality, quality, sustainability, price, delivery speed, convenience, customer service, appearance, etc.? Make sure this aligns with your brand image and marketing strategy.

4. **Behavioral Strategies** — If customers are not currently buying your products, you are going to have to *create* that need or desire. You are going to have to change their current behaviors to be something that directs them to your product. Some strategies can include:

   - **Modeling:** "Celebrity" endorsement or product placement puts the product in the view of customers while being associated with people that they already admire for different reasons. For example: If Serena Williams (tennis player) appears in an advertisement drinking Gatorade, will the customer start to think that Gatorade must be the drink to have if they want to be a serious athlete? Product placement on the other hand is a little more subtle. Think about a TV show, movie, or live event you've ever watched. If you noticed a brand name car, drink, designer, computer, phone, etc., it is likely that the owner of that brand paid to have their product used at that moment. It's not a coincidence that Bumblebee from the movie, Transformers, is a Chevrolet Camaro (and most other recognizable cars are made by GM). Or have you noticed that your favorite sports star might be wearing a certain brand of shoe, or happens to be drinking from a Powerade bottle during their post event interview? Note that a "celebrity" can be someone who is simply: well-known, admired, popular, or followed (social media) by your target market. Who are the influencers of your target market?

> "Fail hard, fail fast, fail often. It's the key to success. This one I learned from experience!"
>
> Reshma Saujani
> CEO & Founder of Girls Who Code

- **Reframing:** Sometimes you will need to take a belief about a product and change it into something that the customer can feel better about. Think about the "Diet" soda concept. There was an attempt to reframe soda, which is considered an unhealthy product, as something which could now be considered healthy just because of people's association of the word "diet" with "healthy." What are the "buzz" words that people want to buy now? Examples could include: organic, sustainable, non-gmo, gluten-free, made from recycled materials, environmentally friendly, locally sourced.

- **Emotion:** Will your advertisement stir the emotions of the customer and push them to buy your product? Advertising which aims to inspire, shame, give hope, invoke guilt, build confidence, etc. can be a strong tool for moving viewers to become buyers. Being good parents, taking care of the environment, helping the underprivileged, looking after our health, and comparing to those around us. These are all examples of topics which can evoke different emotional responses in a viewer, which may in turn cause them to consider buying the product or service.

    F.O.M.O.—Short for Fear of Missing Out. If you can create a scarcity mindset that there are only a limited number of the product, or that it will only be available for a limited time, people can be moved to buy based on not wanting to miss out on something potentially good. This is a play on people's fear or insecurity. A limited time sale on price is another great example of this.

    Y.O.L.O—Short for You Only Live Once. This is another way of playing on a person's fear of missing out. You aim to convince the customer that there's no need defer the reward of buying the product now, since they have no guarantee that they will be able to get it or do it in the future due to the unpredictability of life.

- **Crowd Mentality:** Create the impression that this is the new fad and everyone else is going to buy it too. In doing this you'll create a need in the customer to align with the norm. Make your product or service seem like it's the normal thing to do or have, and customers will be more likely to buy into the idea that they need it too.

- **Skill Acquisition:** Show people how easy it is to do a skill that previously seemed impossible for the average person in your target market. Companies such as Wix.com emphasize how simple website making can be with their product, or TD Ameritrade emphasizes how anyone can get into stock market investing using their product. In other words, that these are skills no longer reserved for the elite or highly educated, because of their product.

- **Convenience and Bundling:** This aims to convince the buyer that they are getting a deal by buying from you. They are getting something extra in terms of service, convenient or premium access, or additional perks for using your product or service. This can be a good time to partner with another business to offer a perk for buying your product. They get to benefit from your advertising, while you get to offer something additional to your product that maybe competitors are not offering.

MARKETING & SALES

BUSINESS ACTIVITY 16
AWARENESS

What is your advertising budget? Where is this money coming from? What are some ways you could reduce advertising costs, but still reach your target market?

Evaluate 4 different media channels that you are considering using from Business Activity 15. What are the advantages and disadvantages of each?

MEDIA CHANNEL	COST	ADVANTAGES	DISADVANTAGES

What parts of your product or service do you plan to showcase in your advertising campaign?

What behavioral strategies do you plan on using in your advertising (modeling, reframing, emotion, crowd mentality, skill acquisition, convenience and bundling)? Give specific examples.

STUDENT WORKBOOK | 53

SECTION 8

> "Entrepreneurship is a habit that you need to practice daily like working out, eating healthy, or getting a good night's sleep. Once you get used to taking action every day, those small wins will compound on each other and move you forward."
>
> **Julie Berninger**
> Creator of Millennial Boss Blog and co-owner of Gold City Ventures

Interest

By now your customer has heard about you, and they are curious enough to want to know more. They could be pausing at your store front, reading beyond the headline of your poster, stopping to listen to you describe your product, visiting your website or social media page, or sending you an email/text/phone call/social media message to check it out further.

You've planted the seed in the customer that "this is something I could potentially want." Now it's important to make sure that there are systems in place to allow the customer to build on their curiousity, develop an interest, and get closer to the point of buying your product.

Information

Is there a way for the customer to learn more about your product or service? Have you included more detailed information about your product or service in your advertisement? Alternatively, are there instructions on how to find out more through places such as a website, social media page, or listed contact information?

- **Pamphlet or Business Card:** Can you give the customer information they need on paper?
- **Website:** Website building has never been easier to do and there are numerous resources available for free and for a fee. These can teach you the basics you need to build a website for your business. Some resources to explore are: Wix, Weebly, Google Sites, and WordPress. All have "How-to" videos on their websites or on YouTube. If you are interested in building a more powerful website and willing to pay for it, there are lots of hosting sites that can be relatively cheap and sometimes come with a free domain name. Find more resources at www.thesimplestartup.com/resources.
- **Social Media Page:** While you can certainly advertise using your personal social media page, it can often be beneficial for a business to have an official business page/account that you can direct customers to if they want to learn more. Just remember that this page is the public face of your business and should not have personal posts.

Some of the most popular social media sites can be used in different ways:

Facebook
A Facebook business page is a useful tool because you can store a lot of information about your business on the page, attract a following of potential customers who like your page, and it easily allows others to share your page if they "like" your product, service, or content you post.

A Facebook business page has some interesting features for your followers, such as allowing them to:

- Post a review of your business.
- Message your business if they want to contact you.

- Post recommendations/feedback on your page.
- Share posts about your content with friends, tag friends in pictures, or tag the business in pictures that they post of themselves using your product/service.

Your Facebook business page has some really useful tools for your business. These include:

- Analyze your 'page insights' to see how many people engage with each post. This should allow you to figure out what types of advertisements people most like and respond to.
- Fill in the "About Us" section to share your business information.
- Conduct market research of your existing followers using tools such as polls, posting links to surveys, allowing for comments on questions, asking for responses using the different emotional response buttons (Like, Love, Laugh, Angry, Sad).

Twitter
A Twitter business account runs the same way as a personal one. Make sure your "handle" aligns with the business name. Unlike Facebook, you will not be able to display much information about the business for customers to find, but it can be used to direct them to your website or other sources of information.

Innovative ways to use Twitter:

- Encourage customers to follow you by providing information about your product, but also consider including information about the industry your product is in. For example, if you are selling home-harvested honey, you might want to Tweet about the bee-keeping industry, local agriculture, how-to care for bees, information about bees, etc. Producing valuable content is a great way to get people to follow your page. You can place sporadic advertisements or pictures of your products within your posts. No one really wants to just be bombarded with advertisements all the time.
- Create a unique hashtag that can be linked to your business and encourage customers to use it when talking about your product. Encourage use of it by highlighting certain customers or having prizes for tagging the business.
- Engage with and support other businesses in your area who might be willing to highlight you back!

Instagram, Pinterest, and Snapchat
While potentially less informative than some of the other platforms, these platforms can be great for attracting followers to your business. Providing content which informs, entertains, builds a relationship, and encourages customers is a great way to utilize these types of media alongside other platforms.

SECTION 8

> "Entrepreneurs have a great ability to create change, be flexible, build companies and cultivate the kind of work environment in which they want to work."
>
> **Tory Burch**
> Founder and CEO of Tory Burch

YouTube

A YouTube business channel can be a great tool if used correctly. Creating content which showcases your product using your advertising strategy and then following up with videos that informs customers more can be a winning play. The videos you create can also be shared across your other platforms too. Live video streaming is not unique to YouTube, but this can be a great way to engage with your customers, answer questions, and give them more reason to get closer to buying your product/service.

General rules to follow across all social media platforms are:

- Keep a relatively high level of engagement with your customers. This means posting content on a regular basis (you can schedule posts to go out at regular time increments in some cases) and be responsive to customer questions, comments, tags, business references, and complaints.

- Keep your content predominantly informative with advertising sprinkled throughout.

- Don't post material which is likely to alienate, annoy, or disturb your target market.

- Be personable and yourself when posting. It's okay to show that you're a human being running this business!

- Keep information posted across platforms consistent, especially if different team members are handling different platforms. Proofread all posts before sending them out. Misspellings and bad grammar can easily be translated by customers to mean a "bad business".

Desire

Your customer knows you're here, they have stopped to learn more, and now it's time to really create that want/need to have your product or service. We are transitioning from the marketing aspect of the business to the sales aspect of the business. At this point, you are in communication with the customer. They have subscribed to your email list, liked or followed your social media account, bookmarked your website, or reached out directly to you. What reason can you give your customer that they should include this product or service in their life? What are your main selling points that apply to the customer? Can you build a trusting relationship where the customer feels like you are serving their interests too?

BUSINESS ACTIVITY 17
INTEREST AND DESIRE

What content can you send out to your customers that might be of interest to them in addition to your advertisements?

What digital media is your business using? Include URLs or other identifying information.

MEDIA TYPE	TITLE	LINK, USERNAME, HANDLE
Website:		
Social Media 1:		
Social Media 2:		
Social Media 3:		

What are the team members' roles in your business advertising strategy? Outline the responsibilities of each person.

What printed media are you planning to use? Include copies* of any business cards, flyers, posters (picture), pamphlets, newspaper advertisements, etc.

* Also include copies of any printed media in Section 8: Appendices of you Business Plan.

SECTION 8

"You are better off trying something and having it not work and learning from that than not doing anything at all."

Mark Zuckerberg
Cofounder of Facebook

Action

This is your final push to the customer to make the decision to purchase your product or service. It's very important at this moment to have clear, convenient ways for the customer to get from where they are (website, social media, poster) to the point of sale. Examples of this are:

- **In person:** You are able to inform the customer of the price and take payment immediately.

- **Online sales:** Have a link that takes your customer directly to the website where they can make a purchase of your product. At this point you may be giving them a place to order a product and information on how to pay you. You can take cash, provide a link to directly pay using credit cards, or give instructions on how to pay you digitally using services such as Apple Pay, Venmo, PayPal, Zelle, etc.

- **A phone number to call:** Give them a number they can call right now to place an order. Be careful of posting your personal information online or in public places. You may want to consider creating a Google Voice or Skype number to use for your business.

- **Email:** Create an email address for your business such as [business name]@gmail.com. Make sure you are checking emails regularly so that you can close the sale as soon as possible after the customer indicates interest.

- **Order Form:** Can your customer complete an order form and pay with cash, check, or credit card? Taking credit cards or checks will require having a bank account for your business where you can deposit a check. If you are considering running a service such as a recreational or educational camp/clinic, this could be the preferred option for signup and/or payment for the customer.

The most important part to this step is having as few barriers and obstacles for the customer to overcome as possible. After all the hard work put in to get them ready to take action, you don't want to lose it because the customer doesn't see the action needed to make the purchase as being worth the effort. Simplicity and convenience are paramount!

MARKETING & SALES

BUSINESS ACTIVITY 18
ACTION

What are the ways that a customer is going to be able to purchase your product/service, once they decide that they want it? Describe the buying process for the customer.

SECTION 9
Cost, Price, Profit

From your previous work on market research (Section 4) and marketing mix (Section 7), you should have already considered the price of your product. This should be based on what you believe your target market is willing to pay for it and what competitors are selling comparable products/services for. However, it is important to dig deeper into the financial side of your business to determine how you will figure out the correct amount to charge which covers your costs, makes a profit, and aligns with your advertising strategies.

Total Cost of Production

When you begin to break down how much it actually costs you to produce your product or service, it is important to make sure you are considering ALL of the costs that go into the process. This includes the costs of labor, all the materials, promotion costs, production costs, packaging, all the way to the final sale. You need to know the **total cost of production** to allow you to set a price for your products and services. The price and total cost of production will be used in determining the profit from each sale and how many units you will need to sell before your business starts making a profit.

When calculating the total cost of your business, there are two main components: fixed costs and variable costs. Their sum amounts to the total cost of the business/product/service.

Total Costs = Fixed Costs + Variable Costs

Fixed Costs are the costs that your business incurs regardless of whether you make any products/provide any services or not. They include up front costs such as: equipment, business entity set up, advertising expenses, website setup, or promotional material (flyers, pamphlets, posters, flags, tents, uniforms). Recurring costs such as: rent, electricity, water, gas, internet, cell phone bill, employee wages, automobile payments, insurance, equipment rental, contractors, or regular maintenance of equipment, are also included in your fixed costs since they will continue to occur whether you are actively engaged in your business or not.

Variable Costs are costs which increase or decrease depending on the level of activity in your business. These can include the costs associated with producing a single unit of your product or performing a single service. Things to consider are: materials, hourly wages, packaging, wear on tools/equipment/automobiles, storage, or gas.

"It doesn't matter how great your original product or idea is, if you can't build a great company, then your product will not endure."

Brian Chesky
Cofounder of Airbnb

60 | THE SIMPLE STARTUP

COST, PRICE, PROFIT

Total Cost Per Unit

An important number to know is the cost per unit of your business. This represents all costs, fixed and variable, divided by the number of products you produce or services you perform.

Total cost per unit (single product or service) can be calculated as follows:

$$\text{Total Cost per unit} = \frac{\text{Fixed Costs}}{(\text{number of units})} + \text{Variable Cost per unit}$$

Naturally, the total cost per unit gets lower as you produce a higher quantity of products or services, because you are dividing the fixed costs by a larger number of units. This isn't always linear, of course. There will be points where you decide to increase or upgrade your equipment, get more space, or hire more employees. This can result from an increase in production demand or increasing the efficiency of the production process.

When thinking about your fixed costs for the business, try a couple of different models where you start with fewer costs, and then as you project to sell more units, try adding in different things that will help your business grow. In the example below, the owners of Sweet Treats experimented with adding in the cost of getting uniform t-shirts printed, getting a custom sales booth made, and building a website.

A good rule to follow is to over-estimate your costs, and under-estimate your sales to make sure the business is going to be profitable.

ITEM	DESCRIPTION	TOTAL
Fixed Costs	Pans, Mixing Bowls, Electricity (estimated), Custom made sales booth, website fee, uniforms	$149
Brownie Costs	Total ingredients costs divided by number of brownies produced per batch (12)	$0.21
Cookie Costs	Total ingredients costs divided by number of cookies produced per batch (20)	$0.16

Projected Sales	Based on market research, about 140 cookies and 50 brownies	190 units

Total Cost per unit, Brownie ⇒ $\frac{149}{190} + 0.21 = \$1.00$ Total Cost per unit, Cookie ⇒ $\frac{149}{190} + 0.16 = \$0.95$

SECTION 9

BUSINESS ACTIVITY 19
TOTAL COST PER UNIT

How many units do you predict you will sell in the coming month? What is this number based on?

_____

_____

Calculate the fixed costs of your business. Any annual costs or single-expense costs should be included in your fixed costs.

FIXED COST DESCRIPTION	PRICE ($)
Total Fixed Costs	

Calculate the variable cost of producing each unit of product or service.

Product/Service 1 - _____

DESCRIPTION OF VARIABLE COST	VARIABLE COST ($)
Total Variable Costs for Product/Service 1	

62 | THE SIMPLE STARTUP

COST, PRICE, PROFIT

Product/Service 2 - _____

DESCRIPTION OF VARIABLE COST	VARIABLE COST ($)
Total Variable Costs for Product/Service 2	

Product/Service 3 - _____

DESCRIPTION OF VARIABLE COST	VARIABLE COST ($)
Total Variable Costs for Product/Service 3	

Calculate the total cost per unit for each of your products/services using the given formula.

$$\text{Total Cost per unit} = \frac{\text{Fixed Costs}}{\text{(number of units)}} + \text{Variable Cost per unit}$$

PRODUCT/SERVICE	CALCULATIONS	TOTAL COST ($)
1.		
2.		
3.		

STUDENT WORKBOOK

SECTION 9

> "If you want to change this world, this community that we all live in, then get up and do it. And just start something."
>
> Anne Wojcicki
> CEO & Co-Founder of 23andMe

Setting the Price

As soon as you have an understanding of how much each unit of your business is going to cost, your pricing strategy can come into play. The amount you charge is going to be one of the most important parts in the success of your business and it may change over time based on feedback from customers. There are many different ways to determine a price for your product:

Cost Plus Pricing – In this strategy, you take the cost of a single unit of the product or service and add a fixed percentage to the cost, such as 50%. This allows you to easily determine the price on different products or levels of service. ($10 Production Costs, Sells for $15)

Competitive Pricing – Based on your market research, what are your competitors charging? In this strategy, you price your product or service in relation to your competition. You need to decide if you are going to be the cheapest option for customers, the most expensive, or fit somewhere in among the pack while relying on other selling points to attract customers to you.

Loss Leaders – Do you have multiple products or services to sell? If so, you might consider selling one of your products at the cost price or even below it. Businesses do this to attract customers to the business in the hope that they will then be tempted to buy more once they are there. This can be a risky strategy however, and should be approached with caution since you have no guarantee that a customer will buy more than the low priced product they came in for. Grocery stores are great examples of this type of pricing. They sell some everyday items, like bread or milk, at a loss, with the aim of getting customers into the store where they will then buy more than just milk or bread.

Penetration Pricing – Set your price low to start, get customers in and loyal to your brand, and then start increasing it slowly to where you really want it to be. This gives you an advantage over your competitors and gets you a market share before becoming less attractive on price. A recent example of this is Apple setting the price point of Apple TV+ much lower than competitors like Disney+ and Netflix. This was with the aim of getting people to subscribe to the service and then stick with it as they increase the price over time.

Price Leadership – When you know you've got a monopoly or USP that sets you above your competitors and you demand the price to match it. You set your price higher than the competition and give the impression to the customer that your product or service is worth it. We see this most in high end brands such as Rolex, Gucci, or Ferrari.

Price Discrimination – Will you offer special pricing or discounts to veterans, teachers, or students in your school? This strategy has you set your price for the general public, but then you have considered a special price for some of the different groups you serve. This is done in the hope that you'll get a higher volume of sales to counterbalance the reduced price to preserve profits.

Break-even Pricing – Businesses who are not necessarily interested in making a profit, but rather just need to cover the costs of the business, might consider setting their price at the minimum needed to cover the total cost of unit production. Non-profit businesses often operate in this way.

Break-even Analysis

A break-even analysis is used by the business to identify the number of unit sales that is needed before the business starts making a profit. The point at which a business is neither losing money or making a profit is referred to as the break-even point.

To calculate the break-even point of a business, divide the total fixed costs of the business by the difference between the price of a single unit and the variable cost to produce it.

Break-even Chart

A break-even chart is used to visually display the financial parts of your business as you sell more units and key points such as the break-even point, fixed costs, variable costs, total income, total costs, margin of safety, loss, and profit.

$$\text{Break-even Point} = \frac{\text{Total fixed costs}}{\text{Unit price - variable cost per unit}}$$

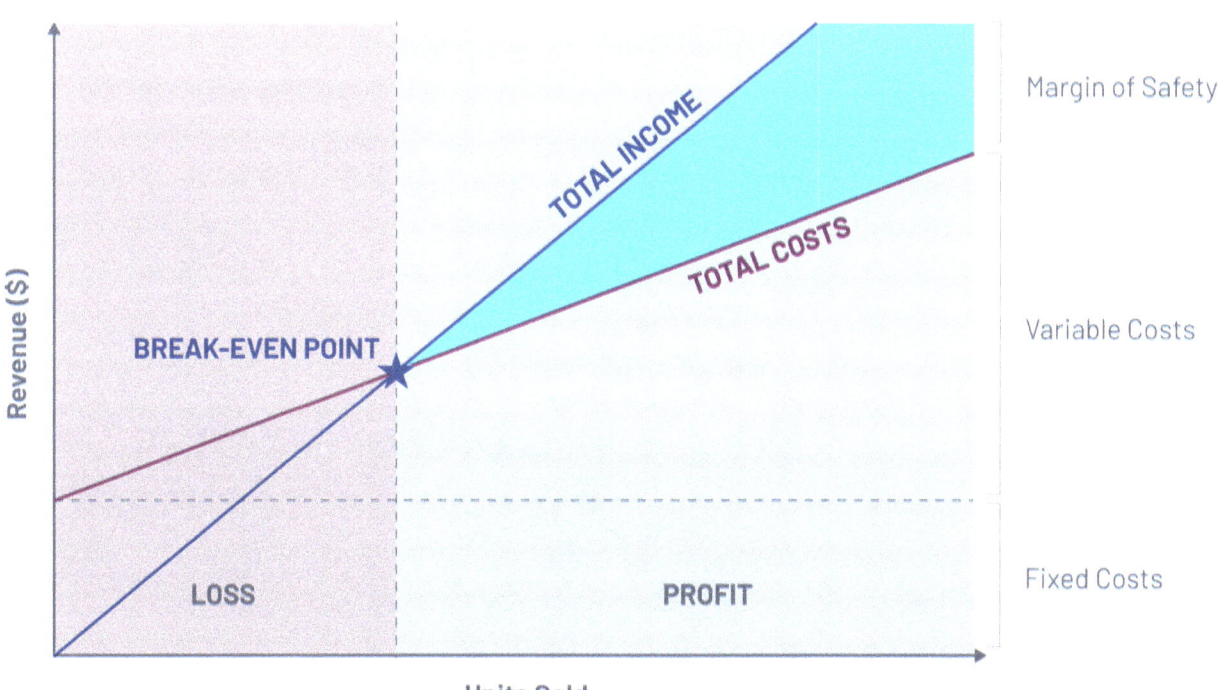

SECTION 9

When you begin to make the break-even chart for your business, it is helpful to use the average of your products, both in cost and sales price, to get a rough estimate of your break-even point. For example, if you have 2 products, A and B, and product A costs $10 to produce and sells for $14, and product B costs $30 to produce and sells for $40, the average cost of your products is $20 and the average selling price is $27. When making your chart, set up your "Revenue" and "Units Sold" axis to be measured in units relative to your business.

Margin of Safety

This is the amount your sales can fall by, before you hit the break-even point. For your business, the goal will be to create a large margin of safety as fast as possible. This allows you, the owner(s), to start taking some of the profits of the business for yourselves.

Example for Sweet Treats Baked Goods

PRODUCT	VARIABLE PRODUCTION COST	TOTAL COST PER UNIT	PRICE (PRICE LEADERSHIP STRATEGY)
Brownies	$0.21	$1.00	$2.00
Cookies	$0.16	$0.95	$1.50
Average of Products	$0.19	$0.98	$1.75

Total Fixed Costs = $149

$$\text{Break-even Point} = \frac{149}{1.75 - 0.19} = 96 \text{ units sold}$$

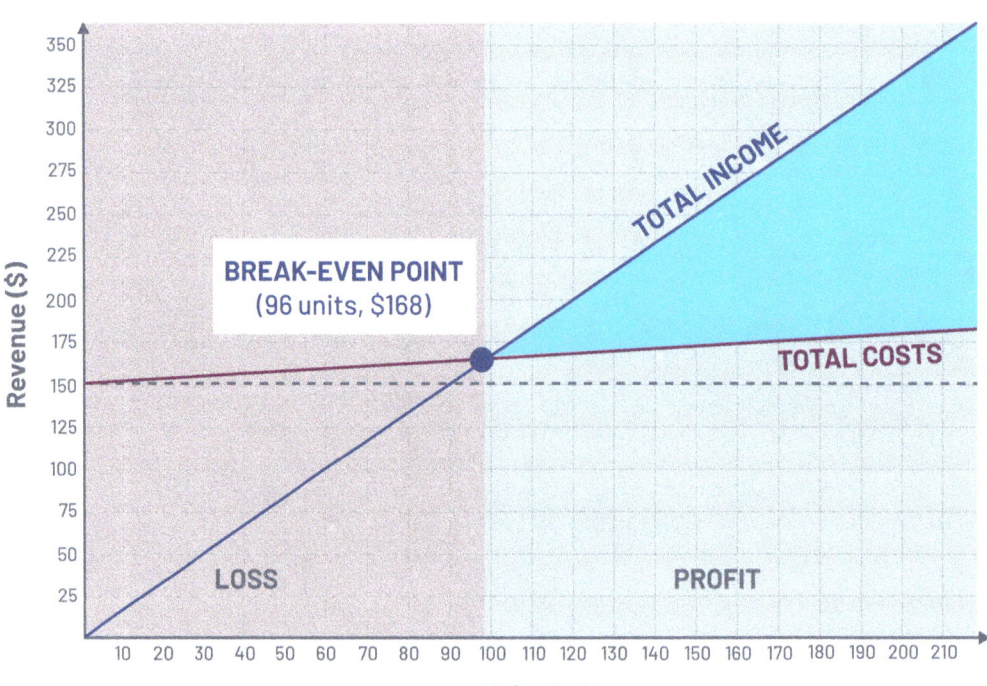

COST, PRICE, PROFIT

BUSINESS ACTIVITY 20
PRICING

What pricing strategy or strategies are you using to determine the price of your product(s) and/or service(s)? Why did you choose this strategy?

List your products or services and the prices you plan on charging for each.

PRODUCT/SERVICE DESCRIPTION	PRICE ($)

Are your prices supported by your market research? Do you feel that this business is still going to be a profitable idea? If yes, explain why you think this. If not, what can you change to encourage the business to be profitable?

STUDENT WORKBOOK | 67

SECTION 9

BUSINESS ACTIVITY 21
BREAK-EVEN ANALYSIS

What is the break-even point of your business? Use averages of your products or services, for your sales price and variable cost per unit, if needed.

$$\text{Break-even Point} = \frac{\text{Total fixed costs}}{\text{Unit price} - \text{variable cost per unit}}$$

Create a break-even chart for your business. In your chart you need to label the key points: *break-even point, fixed costs, variable costs, total income, total costs, margin of safety, loss, profit.*

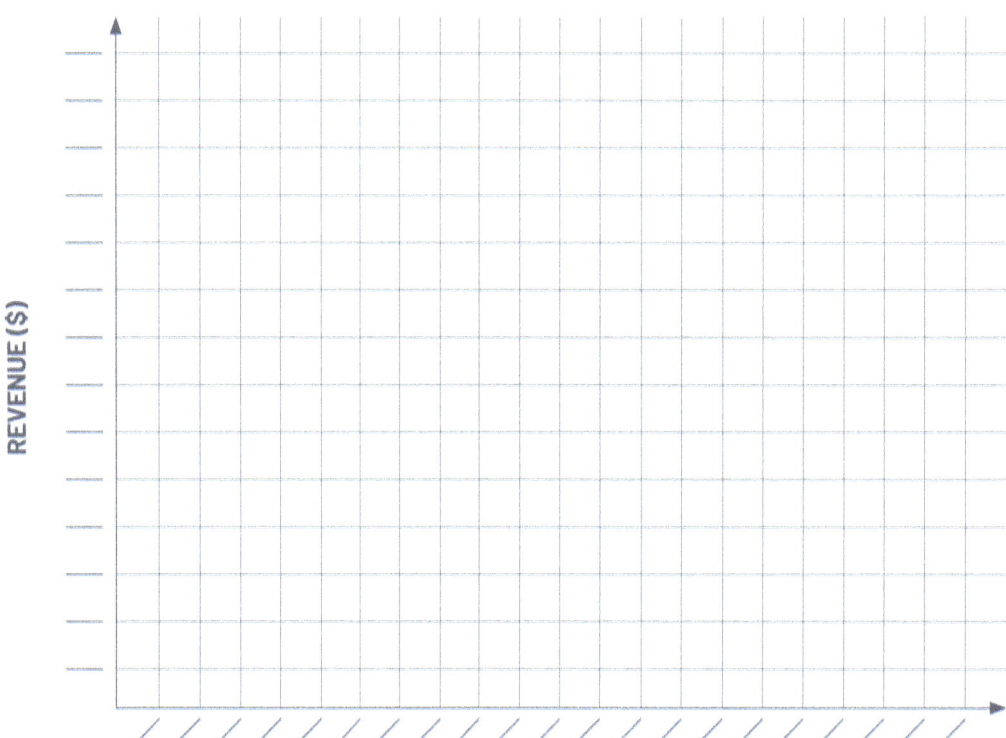

REVENUE ($)

UNITS SOLD

COST, PRICE, PROFIT

"Be brutally honest about the short term and optimistic and confident about the long term."

Reed Hastings
Founder and CEO of Netflix

SECTION 10
Financing

Financing is the money that will be used to:

a) start your business, and
b) cover the operation expenses as you go.

Your aim should be to build a business idea that has very low equipment, material, external labor, and rental costs. BUT, if your business does need some money to get it up and running, what are you going to do?

You have a two main options:

Internally-funded: Each member of the business contributes their own money towards buying the necessary materials, equipment, advertising, rental space, etc. As the business starts to make money, you develop a plan to return the initial cash investment to the person(s) who put it in.

Externally-funded: This involves getting money from an external source, called an investor, to get your business started. Then you will pay back the investor at an agreed-upon schedule for a set amount.

Before approaching an external investor for money, you need to have a completed business plan, accompanied by a market research backed Cashflow Forecast, Cashflow Statement, and Profit/Loss Income Statement. They will look for these to see that the business will be a good investment for them with a high chance of them getting their money back, plus interest.

The most common external investors are:

- **Family members and friends:** Create a proposal where you agree upon how much money is going to be borrowed, when you will pay it back, and if there will be interest included.

- **Banks:** The bank will draft the proposal for the amount, time, and interest rate based on the amount you requested and the strength of your business plan. The more risky an investment seems to a bank, the higher the interest rate they will charge or they will refuse to give you a loan.

- **Venture Capitalists and Angel Investors:** These businesses or individuals provide start-up capital (money) to new businesses that might be struggling to get banks to give them a loan. Businesses can also be interested in the experience and network that comes with a particular investor. The tradeoff may be that you will give up part ownership of the business. For example, if your business is potentially going to be worth $1000, the investor may offer $200 of capital in exchange for 20% ownership of the business. So now the investor is entitled to 20% of the profits of the business, even after they have earned back their initial investment.

> "Entrepreneurship is the path to a life where you're in control of your money and your time. Where you can work when you want and not when you don't feel like it. It's the fastest path to living a life on your own terms. Be your own boss and you'll never get bossed around!
>
> **Grant Sabatier**
> Author of Financial Freedom
> & creator of MillennialMoney.com

Zero-Dollar StartUp

A challenge that you should issue your business is to start it and then grow it with $0 invested of external or internal investment. This can often be referred to as organically growing a business. This is where the profits of the business are enough to fund the next stage of growth. It can be a slower process than you might get using an investor or putting in your own money, but you have almost no risk, because you won't owe anyone money or lose your own money if the business fails. Here are some common ways to get your business off the ground with little to no expense on your part:

1. **Get stuff for free!** Ask yourself, what can I get or do for free that will help my business move forward? This may require some creative thinking, but start with an internet search for: "How do I get _____ for free." You will be surprised at the materials people are giving away (close to expiration, slightly damaged, old model) that you will be able to make use of temporarily; until your business brings in money that you can use to buy better materials. A great example of this is getting a free website for your business using programs such as Wix, Weebly, or Google Sites.

2. **Borrow instead of buy.** If you need tools, equipment, a table, utensils, etc., can you borrow them from someone who has them already? It doesn't have to be for a long period, but just long enough to get through your first batch of sales so that you can go and buy your own. For example, if you are going to build bird houses and sell them, can you borrow the saw, hammer, paint brushes, clamps needed to manufacture them for the first few bird houses and then buy your own tools with the revenue made?

3. **Exchange of Services.** What do you, your team, or your business have that other businesses may want? Can you provide a product to a different business or individual in exchange for a service or product of theirs? Do you need to print some advertisements for your business? How about asking the printing business if they would be willing to lower the price if they are allowed to advertise on the flyers too? Or, do other businesses you know need advertising as well and you can get yours for free by facilitating and designing a shared flier for everyone else? Could you offer one free night of babysitting in exchange for a web designer to build you a website?

4. **Pre-sell your business.** Are you producing a product where you can get your customer to pay you ahead of time for it, and then use the money to buy the material and tools needed? Same thing with a service. Get potential clients to book you ahead of time and pay either in full or a deposit, and then use the money to get your materials. If your business is baking cupcakes, can you pre-sell 2-dozen cupcakes for $1 each and use the $24 to buy the ingredients and cupcake tins? If you are looking to start a car-wash business you can get 5 bookings ahead of time and use the money to buy your sponges, soaps, rags, etc.

5. **Crowdfunding.** An exciting new way for businesses to get off the ground, especially if they can't afford to build a prototype of their product for potential investors to see. Websites such as Kickstarter, Indiegogo, and Go Fund me are

SECTION 10

BUSINESS ACTIVITY 22
STARTUP FUNDING

How much capital are you going to need to start your business?

Where is the money needed to produce your product or provide your service going to come from?

What tools, resources, materials, and labor are you able to get for free or at a dramatically reduced price? Can this be a continuing relationship or is it a one time deal?

What are some ways you'd like to organically grow your business in the future once you start generating revenue?

What other strategies can you use to help reduce the costs of starting up your business?

platforms where you can share your idea and people interested in seeing this idea come to fruition may decide to contribute. They can invest for no benefit, for first access, or in return for a free product.

Cashflow Forecast

Before you approach an investor for money OR put your own money into a business, you need to sit down on your own or with team members and attempt to predict the costs and revenue for your business. This needs to be more than a wild guess. Based on your research and product development, how many units do you predict you are going to sell in the first week, second week, second month, sixth month? As your sales increase, how will your costs change? Will you benefit from buying materials in bulk or save time developing products/services in larger quantities? Make sure these are built into your model.

A cashflow forecast should be structured based on expected income and expenses in each given time period, and those should be broken down by item so there is a clear transparency about what the financials of the business are expected to look like. This is essentially the budget for your business. You should predict out as far as one year. Every month or 3 months (quarter), revisit your predictions and see how they compare to your actual performance and then adjust predictions based on what you currently know about the trends in your market.

Make sure you are describing and referencing the research or assumptions used in coming up with your numbers. Your actual research should be included in your appendices of your business plan.

> "In terms of achievement, the pride is very important to me. It keeps me going every day. The money is always second to me."
>
> **Weili Dai**
> Co-founder of Marvell Technologies

TIME	WEEK 1	WEEK 2	WEEK 3	WEEK 4	TOTAL
Number of Unit 1 Sold					
Number of Unit 2 Sold					
Income					
Investor Income					
Sales Income					
A) Total Income					
Expenditure					
Expense 1					
Expense 2					
Expense 3					
B) Total Expenditure					
C) Income - Expenditure (A-B)					
Opening Balance (previous week closing balance)					
Closing Balance					

Example for Sweet Treats Baked Goods

TIME	WEEK 1	WEEK 2	WEEK 3	WEEK 4	TOTAL
Number of cookies sold ($1.50)	0	40	52	65	157
Number of Brownies sold ($2.00)	0	12	24	33	69

INCOME	WEEK 1	WEEK 2	WEEK 3	WEEK 4	TOTAL
Investor Income	$80.00	$0.00	$0.00	$0.00	$80.00
Sales Income	$0	$84.00	$126.00	$163.50	$373.50
A) Total Income	$80.00	$84.00	$126.00	$163.50	$453.50

EXPENDITURE	WEEK 1	WEEK 2	WEEK 3	WEEK 4	TOTAL
Mixing Bowls	$13.00				$13.00
Cookie Sheets	$14.00				$14.00
Baking Tins	$8.00		$8.00		$16.00
Flour	$7.76				$7.76
Chocolate Chips	$7.30		$7.30		$14.60
Sugar	$6.36			$6.36	$12.72
Eggs	$1.97		$1.97		$3.94
Cacao Powder	$5.99				$5.99
Baking Powder	$4.99				$4.99
Vanilla Extract	$7.36				$7.36
Butter	$2.96		$2.96	$2.96	$8.88
Employee Wage	$0				
Investor Pay	$0	$40	$40		$80
Uniforms	$0			$36.00	$36.00
Sales Booth				$50.00	$50.00
Website				$20.00	$20.00
B) TOTAL EXPENDITURE	$79.69	$40	$60.23	$115.32	$295.24

	WEEK 1	WEEK 2	WEEK 3	WEEK 4	TOTAL
C) Income - Expenditure (A-B)	$0.31	$44.00	$65.77	$48.18	$158.26
Opening Balance (previous week closing balance)	$0	$0.31	$44.31	$110.08	$0
Closing Balance	$0.31	$44.31	$110.08	$158.26	$158.26

BUSINESS ACTIVITY 23
CASHFLOW FORECAST

Create the cashflow forecast for the first 4 weeks of your business. If you have spent money already, back date your forecast to the point in time when you started having expenses and revenue.

TIME	WEEK 1	WEEK 2	WEEK 3	WEEK 4	TOTAL

INCOME	WEEK 1	WEEK 2	WEEK 3	WEEK 4	TOTAL
Investor Income					
Sales Income					
Loan Income					
A) TOTAL INCOME					

EXPENDITURE	WEEK 1	WEEK 2	WEEK 3	WEEK 4	TOTAL
Expense 1					
Expense 2					
Expense 3					
Expense 4					
Expense 5					
Expense 6					
Expense 7					
B) TOTAL EXPENDITURE					

	WEEK 1	WEEK 2	WEEK 3	WEEK 4	TOTAL
C) INCOME – EXPENDITURE (A-B)					
Opening Balance (previous week closing balance)					
CLOSING BALANCE					

Cashflow Statement

As your business grows, you'll need to track all income and expenditure of the business. On a regular basis, you should be comparing this to your cashflow forecast, and then updating the forecast based on what actually happened in the previous time period. If you are going to approach investors to fund the growth of your business, they will be interested in what you predict will happen with the business, but also what has already happened. Can you accurately show how all the money in the business was handled? This gives an insight into the decision making of the business and how your business tends to handle money. Are you going into large debt to fund the business? Are you growing organically? Is there a lot of waste in your materials or over-payment of owners which is stunting the growth of the business?

From a taxation purpose, this is what you will use to pay taxes for the business and what the IRS (US) will look for if your business gets audited. It is extremely important to keep copies of all receipts for expenses and records for sales as evidence of all transactions. Have a system of storing all this information and keeping your cashflow statement up to date.

Your presentation of this will be similar to your cashflow forecast, but can be recorded in different ways. Firstly, you need to track the day-to-day transactions of the business. A template, like the one provided on page 75, will work for most businesses. Talk to an accountant (CPA) about how to handle the taxes for your business.

At the end of the time period (week, month, year) you prepare a summary which is the Cashflow Statement that should go into your business plan. The daily transaction log should be included in your appendices.

Cashflow Log for Sweet Treats

Date	Description	Income	Expense	Balance
Jan 10th	Owner Input from Alan, Mary, Doug	$80		$80
Jan 14th	Supplies: Ingredients		$44.69	$35.31
Jan 15th	Supplies: Baking tins, cookie sheet, mixing bowl		$35	$0.31
Jan 17th	Sales : 20 cookies, 12 brownies	$54		$54.31
Jan 19th	Sales: 18 cookies, 12 brownies	$51		$105.31
Jan 21st	Return investor money Part 1		$40	$65.31

Cashflow Statement for: January 5th—February 3rd	
Opening Balance	$0
Income from sales	$105
Income from other sources	$80
Operating expenses	−$79.69
Repayment of loans/investors	−$40
Closing Balance	$65.31
Profit/Loss (Closing Balance - Opening Balance)	$65.31

SECTION 10

BUSINESS ACTIVITY 24
CASHFLOW STATEMENT

Who is going to be responsible for monitoring the finances of your business? How are they going to do it (notebook, Excel sheet, budgeting software)?

_____

_____

_____

_____

Complete a cashflow log and cashflow statement for the first 4 weeks of your business (or for as long as you've been in operation). Start your cashflow sheet once you've generated income or incurred an expense.

DATE	DESCRIPTION	INCOME	EXPENSE	BALANCE

FINANCING

DATE	DESCRIPTION	INCOME	EXPENSE	BALANCE

Cashflow Statement for: _____ to _____	
OPENING BALANCE	$
Income from sales	$
Income from other sources	$
Operating expenses	$
Repayment of loans/investors	$
CLOSING BALANCE	$
PROFIT/LOSS (CLOSING BALANCE - OPENING BALANCE)	$

Additional copies of the Cashflow Log and Cashflow Statement can be downloaded at *www.thesimplestartup.com/resources*

SECTION 10

> "Everyone makes mistakes but it's how you react and move forward with it that is important."
>
> **Dr. Nora Khaldi**
> Founder of Nuritas

Balance Sheet

This is the equivalent of the **net worth** of an individual for the business. You are going to list all the assets (things owned) and liabilities (money owed) of the business and calculate their worth as if you were going to try and turn them into a cash value today. An investor will be interested in the value of the business as an assessment of risk when investing in your business. If your business has a positive net worth, they are likely to feel more secure that they will get their money back if the business fails and you need to liquidate (turn everything into cash) the business. A good way to go through this process is to imagine that you need to dismantle the business and get as much cash as possible, pay anyone you owe, and then see what's left.

Your assets can include:
- Cash Balance
- Equipment
- Materials
- Stock of your product
- Existing contracts that you have yet to fulfill or be paid for
- Any property belonging to the business
- Vehicles or machinery

Common liabilities are:
- Unpaid bills
- Loans
- Vehicle/Equipment Leases
- Investor payment

The balance sheet for the business should list all of the assets and liabilities of the business, and then subtract the liabilities from the assets to calculate the balance of the business. See the example below for Sweet Treats baked goods.

Balance Sheet for Sweet Treats

Balance Sheet: up to May 31st		
ASSETS		
Cash/Account Balance	$584	
Equipment	$81	Estimated resale value of: Bowls, cookie sheets, baking tin, mixer
Materials	$10	Leftover ingredients
Unsold Product Value	$0	Gave away before they expired
Money Owed	$0	All cookies and brownies were paid for
LIABILITIES		
Unpaid Bills	$0	
Money Owed for loans/investors	$0	Everyone has been paid back
BALANCE (ASSETS - LIABILITIES)	**$675**	$225 per partner if we stop now

80 | THE SIMPLE STARTUP

FINANCING

BUSINESS ACTIVITY 25
BALANCE SHEET

Is keeping a positive balance sheet for your business important to you (your teammates)? Why?

_____

_____

Calculate the current balance of your business.

Balance Sheet: up to _____		
ASSETS		
Cash/Account Balance		
Equipment		
Materials		
Unsold Product Value		
Money Owed		
Other		
Other		
LIABILITIES		
Unpaid Bills		
Money Owed for loans/investors		
Other		
BALANCE (ASSETS - LIABILITIES)		

Does your business currently have a positive balance? What assumptions are you making that might impact the true balance of the business?

_____

_____

_____

SECTION 11
The Pitch

Entrepreneurs often need to present their business to someone. It may be for an entrepreneurship competition, a business expo, or asking potential investors to support your business. It's likely that you are not going to have a huge amount of time to present. Therefore, it's important to make every moment count and convey how great your business is.

If you have not completed your business plan yet, now is the time to do it. Your business plan will be very useful when creating your pitch and will prepare you to be able to answer questions about your business. Use the headings from Section 5 or download the template at www.thesimplestartup.com/resources.

Elevator Pitch

Here's the scenario. You're in an elevator, and in steps a known venture capitalist who likes to invest in businesses such as yours. You can replace the venture capitalist with a bank manager, judge, potential mentor, boss, celebrity, or CEO of a business. The key here is that this is someone who could be very valuable to your business or idea. You need to get your point across to them in the 20-30 seconds that you have with them in the elevator.

This is a short, pre-prepared speech that explains who you are and what your business does in a clear and succinct way. Your pitch needs to be interesting and memorable, but also brief and clear. The other party should end up with a clear idea of what you do and be interested in learning more.

Here are some key stages to developing your elevator pitch:

1. **Identify the purpose of your pitch.** What is the outcome you are looking for from this encounter? Is it to get funding? Are you looking to get hired or hire someone for your business? Do you have an exciting idea for your boss and want permission to work on it? Does this person have connections, products, or services that you would like to use? Or are you simply looking to introduce yourself in an interesting way? Once you identify your goal, everything that goes into your elevator pitch should support this goal and leave out the rest.

2. **The Introduction.** In this stage you need to introduce yourself, your business, and convey the basics of your idea. To keep it as interesting as possible for the listener, focus on the problem you fixed and how you solved it. Make sure that your body language exudes confidence and enthusiasm. If you're not excited about it, why should they be?

3. **Highlight your USP.** What is the Unique Selling Point of your business? Even better, what is the USP that is most likely to interest the person you are talking to? Is it the quality, price, social responsibility, performance, novelty, etc.?

"*Learn the art of the pitch and of messaging.*"

Tim Ferriss
Entrepreneur, Author, Investor, Podcaster

4. **Engage the listener to give you a response.** Throw in a question or a call to action that can't be settled with a simple yes or no answer. Examples: "How does your business currently handle (insert problem)?" or "What product do you like to buy when you are hungry?"
5. **PRACTICE, PRACTICE, PRACTICE.** Your pitch should sound natural and be easy to churn out in an instant.

Prepared Presentation

Maybe your elevator pitch worked and you've secured a meeting to really sell your idea. Or you have an opportunity to present your idea to a judging team and you need to wow them. In this scenario, you may only get about 3-5 minutes to get your information across, but you need to go beyond just getting the listener interested. Now you have to convince them of the merits of your business or idea, and get them to act on it. This action could be engaging the services of your business, putting in a large order of product, funding a growth project, or selecting your business as the best of the array of options presented to them on the day.

You need all the elements of the elevator pitch plus a lot more information, but you want to avoid overwhelming the audience. Here's what to consider before stepping foot into the room or on stage:

- How do you come across to the audience? Venture capitalists and angel investors often claim the leader of a business is as important, if not more important, than the business itself. Do you know your business inside-out? Are you enthusiastic about all aspects of the business? Do you show commitment to the business and the ability to get it past the idea stage? Make sure you practice your presentation in front of the mirror, and if possible a live audience beforehand. Encourage them to give you feedback on your voice, dress, and body language.

- Can you present the essentials of your business in a concise and informative matter? If the other person is interested at the end of the presentation, they will want to see your business plan in full. However, at this point they just want the basic overview.

   You should tell a story in which you briefly highlight:
   - The problem.
   - How you solved it (or plan to solve it).
   - Who your target market is.
   - What research you have conducted.
   - Who your competition is.
   - How you make money.
   - What your current financials look like.
   - What the projections for the future are.

> "Do the one thing you think you cannot do. Fail at it. Try again. Do better the second time. The only people who never tumble are those who never mount the high wire. This is your moment. Own it."
>
> **Oprah Winfrey**
> Founder of Harpo Productions and OWN

SECTION 11

- Consider what visual media you can use to aid you in your presentation. Can you include a slideshow presentation or poster display? Do you have a prototype or samples of your product ready to put in their hands? Is this a service or skill you can demonstrate? Use these visual aides to get more information across. Put your financial details into charts that are easy to interpret.

- What is your plan for the future? While it's very important to have a clear picture of where your business is currently at, it's equally important to share your vision for the future. How do you see the business growing? What are the short-term and long-term goals of the business and what are the steps you plan to take to reach them? If you can include how the listener will play a part in this, even better.

- Who is your audience? What do you know about them already? The more personalized you can make your presentation to the person listening, the more you will build them into the vision of the business. Do your research. What does the person/business already do? What do they need? Know why you are going to be a good solution for them. If presenting to judges, make sure you know what criteria you are being judged on and confirm you are hitting on all the key points.

- Can you answer any question that comes up about your business? Try to predict what questions you might be asked and prepare answers for them. When you practice your presentation on others, what are they typically asking about? Do you know anyone in a similar role to your intended audience, who would be willing to give you feedback on your presentation?

BUSINESS ACTIVITY 26
PRESENTATION

Write a 30-second elevator pitch to someone who knows nothing about you or your business, but could be a potential customer.

For a longer pitch, what visual aids will you use to accompany your presentation? What will they show (image of product, finances, marketing, advertising, etc.)?

VISUAL MEDIA TYPE	INFORMATION REPRESENTED

SECTION 11

What are 3 questions you think a potential customer, judge, investor, or someone evaluating your business might ask you about your business? What would be your responses?

Question 1

Response 1

Question 2

Response 2

Question 3

Response 3

"The leader of a business is as important as the business itself."
How will you convince your listener that you are just as important to the business as the idea?

"If you try one approach, and it doesn't work, then you must try another approach. People will all the time say things like, 'Well, I think I tried everything.' But you didn't. You tried one way, and it didn't work. What about the 14 other ways that you can try, and then the other 14 ways you can try if that doesn't work?"

Cathy Heller
Author of Don't Keep Your Day Job

SECTION 12
Final Review

> "As entrepreneurs, we must continue to ask ourselves "What's Next?"
>
> **Cher Wang**
> Cofounder of HTC Corporation

Congratulations! If you have made it this far you are officially an entrepreneur and small business owner. You've taken an important step in learning how to create income streams for yourself instead of having to rely on working for someone else.

Hopefully you have acquired new skills, made important connections, and learned exciting things about yourself along the way. Even if you don't see entrepreneurship in your future, that doesn't mean you can't take what you've learned here and apply it to your career. Intrapreneurship is when an employee at a company uses the skills of entrepreneurship to solve problems within the business they work for. This can be a great way to earn promotions and fast-track your way into management positions.

As you go through the review section, take your time and reflect both with your teammates and on your own. Discuss experiences, conflicts, differences of opinion, triumphs, failures, lessons learned, etc. Reflect back on earlier sections of this workbook to see the milestones you've completed along the way. If you kept a reflective journal during this process, consult it to see how you felt at different times in the project and compare it to how you feel now.

Please share your experience in starting a business using this workbook and view the stories of other businesses at www.thesimplestartup.com/stories.

FINAL REVIEW

BUSINESS ACTIVITY 27
REVIEW

What did you learn about working with others or working on your own during this project?

What skills and knowledge did you acquire as a result of running your business?

I LEARNED HOW TO...	I LEARNED ABOUT...

What were your top 3 highlights/successes from the project? Why were these important moments for you?

Highlight/Success 1:

Description 1:

Highlight/Success 2:

Description 2

Highlight/Success 3:

Description 3:

SECTION 12

**What were the 3 biggest difficulties and/or challenges you faced during this project?
How did you overcome them?**

Difficulty 1: _____
Solution 1: _____

Difficulty 2: _____
Solution 2 _____

Difficulty 3: _____
Solution 3: _____

**Do you see entrepreneurship as a career path or something you might explore in the future?
What might this look like? If not, how do you see the experience of this project helping you in your future career?**

_____
_____
_____
_____
_____
_____

Did you consider your business to be successful? Why or why not? Did you make a profit? How much?

_____
_____

Is there anything you would change if you were to do this again and start a new business?

_____
_____
_____

FINAL REVIEW

"When you have a passion for something then you tend not only to be better at it but you work harder at it too."

Vera Wang
Founder of Vera Wang

APPENDICES

APPENDIX 1	BUSINESS IDEAS	94
APPENDIX 2	REFLECTIVE JOURNAL	96
APPENDIX 3	FOUNDERS' AGREEMENT	101
APPENDIX 4	TEAM MEETING OUTLINE	104
APPENDIX 5	SAMPLE BUSINESS PLAN	109
APPENDIX 6	RESOURCES	120
APPENDIX 7	GLOSSARY	121
APPENDIX 8	BIBLIOGRAPHY	126

You can download additional copies of most of the appendices at www.thesimplestartup.com/resources

APPENDIX 1
BUSINESS IDEAS

Below are some suggested business ideas to help give you some inspiration.

- Open a student store
- Sell concessions at sports games
- Sell advertising on your YouTube channel
- Create a blog reviewing things you are interested in with affiliate links
- Car washes
- Lawn-mowing service
- Errand driver
- Food delivery
- Coffee service
- Handcrafted goods
- Instructional videos
- Write a blog
- Manage social media for other businesses
- Create graphics for other businesses
- Leaf raking/snow shoveling
- Babysitting
- Tutoring
- Baking specialty cakes
- Organize sporting events
- Teach a class
- Dog walking
- Window cleaning
- Website designer
- Event organizer (birthdays, trips to local attractions, dances)
- Freelance photographer
- T-shirt designer
- Run a camp (sports, drama, music, board games)
- Flip furniture/used appliances/tools/parts/clothing
- Fix computers
- Paint local business windows
- Take junk to the dump or recycling center
- Drop-ship popular items
- Entertainer: musician, magician, stand-up comic
- Referee a sport
- Organize a school play
- Create custom jewelry
- Complete odd jobs for people
- Grow and sell flowers
- Train dogs or horses
- Pet grooming
- Teach English online
- Sell digital services on Fiverr
- House sitting
- Grow and sell fruit/vegetables
- Start a podcast
- Freelance write for a local newspaper or website
- Provide care for the elderly
- Clean pools
- Basic auto maintenance
- Sell your artwork
- Write a comic or ebook
- Be a local tour guide
- Create a brochure of local events, businesses, and attractions
- Answer surveys online
- Organize video game tournaments
- Hand-crafted greeting cards
- Cooking service or lunch service
- Driver (Uber, Lyft, etc.)
- Personal training
- Fix phones

APPENDIX 1: BUSINESS IDEAS

Future Business Ideas

Every time you come up with a new business idea, write it down! You can always come back to your list at a later time and start one of your ideas. Take a couple of minutes to write down a brief outline of any ideas you come up with during this project.

Business Idea Name	Brief Description of the idea (who, what, where, when, why, how).	How easy is this idea to implement? Circle a rank from 1-5 (1 = difficult to start, 5 = really easy to start)
		1 2 3 4 5
		1 2 3 4 5
		1 2 3 4 5
		1 2 3 4 5
		1 2 3 4 5
		1 2 3 4 5
		1 2 3 4 5
		1 2 3 4 5
		1 2 3 4 5
		1 2 3 4 5

STUDENT WORKBOOK | 95

APPENDIX 2
REFLECTIVE JOURNAL 1

Date: _____

This journal is designed to give you a space to reflect on new information you have acquired over the week, whether that be from direct instruction, discussions with people in your life, or research you've conducted on your own. You should use this space to break down that new information, evaluate it for its worth, and then decide how you are going to implement it in your business (if at all). Try to answer all prompts with as much detail as you can give.

Recap on your business week. What steps did you take in developing your business? Did you have any successes or challenges?

_____
_____
_____
_____
_____
_____
_____

What new skills or information did you learn this week? Is this valuable and applicable to your business right now? What will you change about your business (if anything) as a result of what you learned?

_____
_____
_____
_____
_____

What other business ideas have you had since you started the business project? Do you think you'd like to explore any of them in the future?

_____
_____
_____
_____
_____
_____

APPENDIX 2
REFLECTIVE JOURNAL 2

Date: _____

This journal is designed to give you a space to reflect on new information you have acquired over the week, whether that be from direct instruction, discussions with people in your life, or research you've conducted on your own. You should use this space to break down that new information, evaluate it for its worth, and then decide how you are going to implement it in your business (if at all). Try to answer all prompts with as much detail as you can give.

Recap on your business week. What steps did you take in developing your business? Did you have any successes or challenges?

_____
_____
_____
_____
_____
_____
_____

What new skills or information did you learn this week? Is this valuable and applicable to your business right now? What will you change about your business (if anything) as a result of what you learned?

_____
_____
_____
_____
_____

What skill would you like to learn that could help your business be more successful or branch out in a new direction?

_____
_____
_____
_____
_____

APPENDIX 2
REFLECTIVE JOURNAL 3

Date: _____

This journal is designed to give you a space to reflect on new information you have acquired over the week, whether that be from direct instruction, discussions with people in your life, or research you've conducted on your own. You should use this space to break down that new information, evaluate it for its worth, and then decide how you are going to implement it in your business (if at all). Try to answer all prompts with as much detail as you can give.

Recap on your business week. What steps did you take in developing your business? Did you have any successes or challenges?

_____
_____
_____
_____
_____
_____
_____
_____

What new skills or information did you learn this week? Is this valuable and applicable to your business right now? What will you change about your business (if anything) as a result of what you learned?

_____
_____
_____
_____
_____

Could you continue this business into college or after you start a full-time job? If not, can you see yourself creating a side-business to supplement your income? What might it look like?

_____
_____
_____
_____
_____
_____

APPENDIX 2
REFLECTIVE JOURNAL 4

Date: _____

This journal is designed to give you a space to reflect on new information you have acquired over the week, whether that be from direct instruction, discussions with people in your life, or research you've conducted on your own. You should use this space to break down that new information, evaluate it for its worth, and then decide how you are going to implement it in your business (if at all). Try to answer all prompts with as much detail as you can give.

Recap on your business week. What steps did you take in developing your business? Did you have any successes or challenges?

What new skills or information did you learn this week? Is this valuable and applicable to your business right now? What will you change about your business (if anything) as a result of what you learned?

Do you know any business owners or entrepreneurs? What do you think they do well or makes them successful? If possible, go one step further and ask them!

APPENDIX 2
REFLECTIVE JOURNAL 5

Date: _____

This journal is designed to give you a space to reflect on new information you have acquired over the week, whether that be from direct instruction, discussions with people in your life, or research you've conducted on your own. You should use this space to break down that new information, evaluate it for its worth, and then decide how you are going to implement it in your business (if at all). Try to answer all prompts with as much detail as you can give.

Recap on your business week. What steps did you take in developing your business? Did you have any successes or challenges?

What new skills or information did you learn this week? Is this valuable and applicable to your business right now? What will you change about your business (if anything) as a result of what you learned?

Find a blog, website, video blog, podcast, or book that teaches people about being business owners or entrepreneurs. Summarize what it was about and what you learned.

APPENDIX 3
FOUNDERS' AGREEMENT

Business Name: _____

Founders: _____ , _____ , _____ ,

_____ , _____ , _____ ,

The listed names (each a "Founder" and together the "Founders") are collaborating with the purpose of developing together a business with the following description: [briefly describe the purpose and nature of the business idea]

_____

_____

_____

I. Ownership Rights of Created Material

If something is created or contributed for the business such as a material, product, idea, technology, resource, image, name, logo, etc., who owns it during the project and then after the project is completed?

_____

_____

_____

_____

II. Dispersion of Business Profits and Liquidation

Once the business is generating income and the costs to the founders are covered, how will the profits of the company be treated? Will they be reinvested into the business or divided amongst the founders?

_____

_____

_____

_____

At the conclusion of the business, how will you divide the equity of the business? Detail how the business will be broken down and who gets what.

_____

_____

_____

III. Roles and Commitments of Founders

How much time is each person expected to contribute to the business each week? Outline any specific tasks that must be completed by the individual members of the business. Are there obligatory team meetings every week or mandatory attendance at different events?

_____

_____

_____

_____

_____

_____

_____

_____

_____

IV. Initial Contributions

What resources or money are the founders bringing into the business? Detail the different contributions of the founding members.

_____

_____

_____

_____

_____

_____

_____

_____

_____

V. Conflict Resolution, Separation, Cessation of Business

In the event of a dispute between the owners of the business, what will be the steps in resolving the conflict? This can include conflicts regarding decisions about the business or personal differences of opinion. What happens if a founder is not completing their agreed upon duties for the business?

In the event that a founding member no longer wishes to be a part of the business, how will their separation from the business be handled? Will it result in the termination of the business? Will they have to wait until the closing of the business by the other founding members, before being entitled to a share of the business equity? Do they forfeit their share of profits? Will the other members have to buy them out of their perceived portion of the business?

Is it possible for a founding member to be removed from the business by the other members? Can a unanimous or majority vote be used? Must certain criteria be met first? Is the person entitled to notice and a chance to change the behaviors that caused the conflict?

Date of Signed Agreement:

Signatures of agreement of the founders of

APPENDIX 4
TEAM MEETING OUTLINE

Business Name: _____ Meeting #: _____

Date: _____ Time: _____

Attendees Present: _____ , _____ , _____
                   _____ , _____ , _____

Minutes of Meeting

What topics were discussed? What decisions were made? What tasks do attendees have as a result of the meeting? When do tasks need to be completed by?

_____
_____
_____
_____
_____
_____
_____
_____
_____
_____
_____
_____

Next Meeting Date: _____

Next Meeting Location: _____

Topics for Discussion: _____
_____
_____

Signature of Owners or Secretary: _____   Date: _____

APPENDIX 4
TEAM MEETING OUTLINE

Business Name: Meeting #:

Date: Time:

Attendees Present:

Minutes of Meeting

What topics were discussed? What decisions were made? What tasks do attendees have as a result of the meeting? When do tasks need to be completed by?

Next Meeting Date:

Next Meeting Location:

Topics for Discussion:

Signature of Owners or Secretary: Date:

APPENDIX 4
TEAM MEETING OUTLINE

Business Name: _____ Meeting #: _____

Date: _____ Time: _____

Attendees Present: _____ , _____ , _____ ,

_____ , _____ ,

Minutes of Meeting

What topics were discussed? What decisions were made? What tasks do attendees have as a result of the meeting? When do tasks need to be completed by?

_____

_____

_____

_____

_____

_____

_____

_____

_____

_____

Next Meeting Date: _____

Next Meeting Location: _____

Topics for Discussion:

_____

_____

Signature of Owners or Secretary: _____ Date: _____

APPENDIX 4
TEAM MEETING OUTLINE

Business Name: _____   Meeting #: _____

Date: _____   Time: _____

Attendees Present: _____ , _____ , _____ ,

_____ , _____ ,

Minutes of Meeting

What topics were discussed? What decisions were made? What tasks do attendees have as a result of the meeting? When do tasks need to be completed by?

_____

_____

_____

_____

_____

_____

_____

_____

_____

_____

Next Meeting Date: _____

Next Meeting Location: _____

Topics for Discussion:

_____

_____

Signature of Owners or Secretary: _____   Date: _____

APPENDIX 4
TEAM MEETING OUTLINE

Business Name: _____   Meeting #: _____

Date: _____   Time: _____

Attendees Present: _____ , _____ , _____ ,
_____ , _____ ,

Minutes of Meeting

What topics were discussed? What decisions were made? What tasks do attendees have as a result of the meeting? When do tasks need to be completed by?

_____

_____

_____

_____

_____

_____

_____

_____

_____

Next Meeting Date: _____

Next Meeting Location: _____

Topics for Discussion:

_____

_____

Signature of Owners or Secretary: _____   Date: _____

APPENDIX 5
SAMPLE BUSINESS PLAN

Sweet Treats

Business Plan for "Sweet Treats"

June 1st, 2020

123 Enterprise Avenue,

Biz Town, ME, 00000

800-123-4567

sweettreatsbakedgoodsproject@gmail.com

Table of Contents:

Executive Summary	Page 1
Business Overview	Page 2
Market Analysis and Competition	Page 2
Sales and Marketing Plan	Page 3
Ownership and Management Plan	Page 5
Operating Plan	Page 6
Financial Plan	Page 7
Appendices	Page 9

Section 1: Executive Summary

Sweet Treats is a homemade, baked goods business with the aim of providing delicious snack options to the students of StartUp High School. We aim to provide excellent tasting products, made with top quality ingredients, at a price that is competitive and accessible to today's high school student. Our goal is to be the #1 snack option for students and staff during and immediately after the school day, which we will achieve by being one of the few options available and through a fun and exciting marketing campaign.

Sweet Treats is the creation of owners Alan, Mary, and Doug, who came together with the goal of solving the problem of insufficient food options available to students and staff immediately after school. We are equal owners of the business and will share all responsibilities and profits in equal parts. Mary will be the lead person for our marketing strategy. Alan will handle all the finances of the business, including the business bank account, cash box, and payment of vendors. Doug will oversee the production of the product and ensure that we are producing an adequate quantity of product as well as quality control. We will meet on a weekly basis for official team meetings, as well as several informal meetings during the week to ensure the business continues to run and grow as expected.

To begin, Sweet Treats will offer 2 products to customers: chocolate chip cookies and brownies. Our business will operate in the cafeteria 2 days a week after school. Students can pick up pre-ordered products or walk-in and buy from our inventory available that day. We will aim to have top quality customer service that will ensure being very friendly and willing to replace any product that a customer finds legitimate fault with. We eventually would like to start offering our products during after-school events such as home sports games, concerts, plays, and award events. We will also look to form partnerships with other school businesses and the cafeteria to get them to offer our product during times we are not in operation, with a small percentage of the profits going to them. We will also consider expanding our product range to include a greater variety of flavors and baked goods.

At the moment, there is a very limited selection for students or staff who are looking for food immediately after school. Students who might be staying after school include those staying for sports, extended study opportunities, detention, drama, music, clubs, and societies. Our market research indicates that this averages at around 150 students each day and there are additional staff as well. The options for food at the moment include over-priced vending machines with poor selection or a local gas station which is about an 800-yard walk. The distance is a big deterrent to many despite being hungry. There is very limited delivery service in our school's area with most delivery and ride share companies not operating within our town, or charging excessive prices to come out from the nearest city. We believe there is a great opportunity for our business in this current market. We plan to target all the students who are staying after school, but will get the most business from the non-athlete students, based on our market research.

Our intention is to operate our business for the remaining 15 weeks of the school year, originally at 2 days a week, but with the intention of expanding using business partnerships as already mentioned, and exploring the option of hiring workers to produce our products or staff the sales booth on days we are not currently operating. We are currently profitable after 4 weeks of operation, and project to finish with a $1240.00 profit at the end of the 15 week period. This is based on current sales, market research, and customer feedback.

Section 2: Business Overview

Sweet Treats is competing in the food, snack, and convenience food industry. We provide convenient, tasty, affordable home-baked goods for students and staff in StartUp High School. We will provide cookies and brownies, made from high-quality ingredients, in the hour immediately after school, before most students have gone home or started participating in their after-school activities.

The food/snack industry in our school is not very saturated. There are 5 vending machines located in various locations around the school. Of those, 3 provide drink options only. The other 2 provide food options, but these are very limited in selection, are priced at $2 per item for things like candy bars or potato chips, and can often be empty due to not having supplies replaced often enough. This latter information also tells us there is a demand for snack options outside of what students are bringing/buying for lunch. Based on our market research, we believe that students will choose our product over vending machine options because we have a delicious product, a more filling product, the ability to order ahead, and the ability to pay for it using digital payment. The vending machines are cash only.

The local gas station, which is roughly 800 yards away, presents several challenges for students. Students often don't have the time after school to get there and back before their after school activity starts. Our market research shows that students are interested in an option located within the school that is quick and easy to access. The distance of the gas station from the school also challenges students who "don't feel like" walking that far to get a snack. We believe our business will be accessible enough to entice them to become our customer.

The average student in our school spends $3.00 on snacks when they do buy them, and we believe we have a product capable of earning a majority of that $3.00 from each student who stays in the school. We have great products, that are filling, tasty, made with high quality ingredients, easy to get, and ready to walk away with so our customers can get to their activities quickly.

Section 3: Market Analysis and the Competition

Our target market is the 150 students (average day) who have after school activities starting shortly after the end of the school day. Of those, about 50% are athletes who did not seem as interested in our products as the 50% non-athletes. Our market research shows that about 78% of students surveyed are interested in purchasing a snack after school, before their activity starts. If we can capture 75% percent of this, that will put our average day at about 44 customers. Our sales fell short of this number during our first 2 weeks in operation, but the last 2 weeks have shown a steady increase in sales which has already surpassed the target 44 customers per day. Our target market remains the same, but we have also noticed that we are also selling to some athletes, students who walk home from school, or get picked up shortly after the school day ends. We also hadn't considered students from other schools, attending different events, being customers too. As a result, we have made plans for expanding our operation hours to include dates when there are school events. We will either operate a sales booth on those days, or look for existing vendors to sell our product along-side theirs with a profit-sharing model in place.

So far, the average sale per customer has been $1.82, with a total revenue of about $80 per day over the past week. We expect this to continue to grow as awareness of our business grows and our production/hours of operation increases. We believe we are winning a lot of the market share from the vending machines and local gas station and hope to continue to do so with our competitive advantages of product, accessibility, price, and convenience.

Section 4: Sales and Marketing Plan

Product - Our business will produce homemade cookies and brownies made from high quality ingredients. High quality ingredients means that we will be buying all ingredients from local stores with reputable brand-name ingredients, and the simplest ingredient list possible. We want to avoid added preservatives and unnecessary ingredients. We decided to produce cookies and brownies based on our market research. During our research we surveyed 100 students about their preference of baked good based on samples for 5 different cookie flavors (chocolate chip, oatmeal raisin, snickerdoodle, peanut butter, sugar) and also tested brownies, caramel squares, and macaroons to see which product was most popular. Each cookie will be approximately 3 inches in diameter and we include a list of ingredients on our product label. Brownies are 3 inches x 2.5 inches approximately and 3/4 inch high. We find that these portions are large enough for our customers to feel satisfied with a single unit, will provide a satiating snack, can be compared with the quantity of vending machine or gas station snack products. The fresh nature and taste then sets us apart from our competition.

Price - We calculated the cost of producing 1 cookie to be $0.16 based on the total ingredients used to make the dough and then dividing that by 20 cookies which is produced by 1 batch of dough. Brownies were calculated in a similar way with a cost of $0.21 per brownie based on a batch of batter producing 12 brownies. Our total fixed costs, including some growth items such as our website, uniforms, and sales booth, comes to $149. We would like to recuperate all of our fixed costs within the first 4 weeks, and we have conservatively estimated selling 190 brownies and cookies in that time period. We are confident we will surpass that, and currently are on track to do so. Based on the estimated sales, we came to a total cost of production for a single cookie to be $0.95 and brownie to be $1.00. This includes the fixed and variable costs of the business. We decided therefore to set our prices based on a significant profit margin to the total cost of production, and to stay competitive with the vending machines in the school and gas station nearby. Cookies will be sold for $1.50, which gives a $0.55 profit per cookie initially, and a $1.34 profit once our fixed costs have been recovered. Brownies have been priced higher due to the higher cost of production, higher volume per unit, and based on our research which showed that students were willing to pay more for a brownie than a cookie. We have priced our brownies at $2.00 per unit. This gives us a $1.00 profit before fixed costs are recovered, and a $1.79 profit afterwards.

A bag of potato chips from the vending machine can cost between $1.50-$1.75, and it ranges between $1.25-$1.80 in the gas station. A full size candy bar costs $1.25-$ 1.60 in the vending machine and is about the same in the gas station. So while brownies are sold at a higher price than most of our competitors products, our market research tells us our target market will be willing to pay our price for the convenience and quality of the brownie.

APPENDIX 5: SAMPLE BUSINESS PLAN

PRODUCT	VARIABLE PRODUCTION COST	TOTAL COST PER UNIT	PRICE (PRICE LEADERSHIP STRATEGY)
Brownies	$0.21	$1.00	$2.00
Cookies	$0.16	$0.95	$1.50
Average of Products	$0.19	$0.98	$1.75

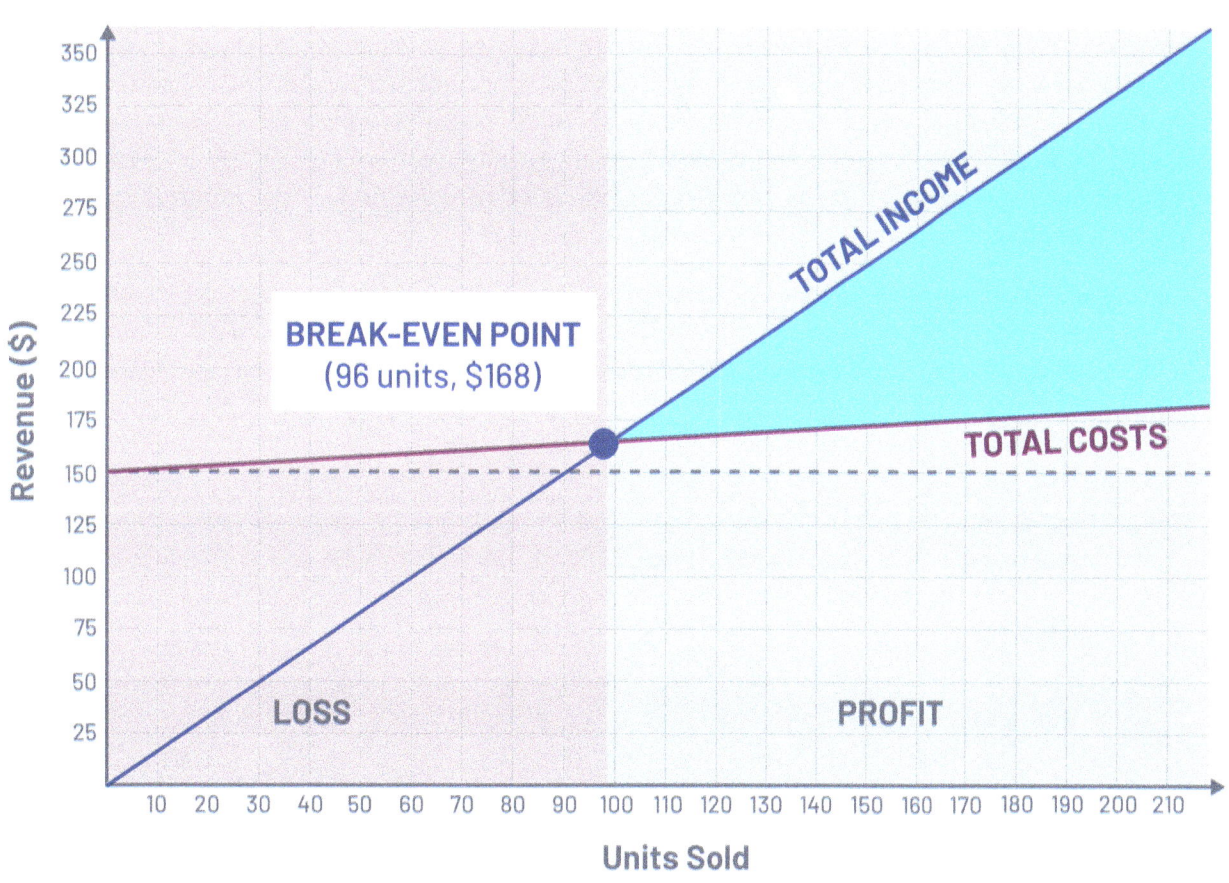

Promotion - We have several methods of promoting our products and business. To start, we will create posters to hang around the hallways which will advertise our business, what we sell, where we will be located, and when we will be selling. After that, we will add a social media Facebook, Twitter, Instagram, and Snapchat profile, which we will encourage students and staff to subscribe to. We will post content about our product, the process of starting a mini-business, and some tips on how to bake. We will look to build a following as fast as possible through some different promotions and interesting content. Once we have been in operation for 3-4 weeks, we plan to buy a domain and build a website to advertise our business information and answer FAQ's from customers. Another project, before our big community craft festival (May 15th) and our school's business expo, is to have a custom sales booth built by an owner's friend. Then we will add custom made uniforms. These elements will complete our professional appearance and hopefully boost sales as we support our high-quality brand image.

Place - We will be setting up a table inside of the cafeteria, twice a week initially, to sell our products. As we grow, we hope to expand the number of days a week our product is available, as well as the number of locations. We plan to have other businesses sell our products and get them placed in sports game food stands, with a profit sharing model for the school. Orders can be done in advance via text or a social media platform, but the point of sale will be in person. Customers will have the option to pay with cash, or via digital payment using apps such as PayPal, Venmo, Zelle, or Apple Pay.

Packaging - Each item we produce will be wrapped in tight polyethylene food wrap. Eventually, we would like to get custom stickers made with our logo on them to improve the appearance of our product, but we have determined that it is not worth the additional cost to begin with and it is something we can add at a later date.

Section 5: Ownership and Management Plan

Sweet Treats will operate as a partnership with all 3 owners retaining equal ownership and responsibility for the business (Alan - 33.33%, Mary - 33.33%, Doug - 33.33%). All members of the group will aim to contribute an equal amount of work and will take responsibility for different aspects of the business. Structure and roles are outlined below.

OWNER	OWNER	OWNER
Alan	Mary	Doug
Financial Manager	**Marketing Manager**	**Production Manager**
■ Track all income and expenses of the business ■ Take responsibility for the cash box and depositing money in business bank account ■ Own the digital payment apps that customers can use to pay for products ■ Reimburse owners for expenses related to the business ■ Make brownies	■ Oversee making of posters ■ Manage social media accounts ■ Order t-shirts ■ Make cookies	■ Oversee rotation of baking duties ■ Buy all ingredients for team ■ Check all products for quality before they are listed for sale ■ Make cookies

To begin with, no other employees or contractors will be needed. We will manage all aspects of the business ourselves. As we grow, we will look to hire additional bakers, sales people, and possibly a website and social media manager. The profits of the business will have to be large enough to support the extra help before we will consider it.

The uniforms will be outsourced to a private t-shirt printing business (TBD). The custom sales booth will be outsourced to Alan's friend, Megan, who likes carpentry and welding, and will build it for us as a very reduced rate if we let her advertise her business on it.

Section 6: Operating Plan

We will locate our business in the school cafeteria to start, but will look to expand into identified areas such as school sports snack shops and the local craft festival which we need to apply for a space to operate, via the event organizers.

The production process for our product includes:

- Buy ingredients
- Make batter or dough
- Bake in oven
- Let cool
- Individually wrap
- Box for transport to the school.

Cookies take approximately 55 minutes to produce per batch. Brownies take about 60 minutes. This includes mixing the dough/batter, putting on the cookie sheet/pan, baking time, and individual wrapping time. Ingredients will be purchased in bulk every other week and will take approximately 25 minutes to get to the local store, buy the ingredients, and get home again.

See recipes for procedure and ingredients in Section 8: Appendices and Exhibits

The amount of cookies and brownies we produce for each sales day will depend on pre-sale numbers, and then we will add at least 1 batch of cookies and brownies for customers who purchase on the day. If it looks like we need to increase production to account for growing demand, we can easily do that through increasing how many we make, or outsourcing batches to employed students.

Our sales booth will consist of a table with a table cloth (borrowed from Doug's parents), a cash box, laminated sign showing our products, prices, social media information, and information on how to pre-order or pay digitally. We were able to laminate our sign in our school library for free.

Equipment needed will include: mixing bowls (x2), baking tin (9"x9"), cookie sheet (x2), whisk (x1), electric mixer (borrowed from parents), spatulas (x3), wax paper, polythene wrap. All can be sourced from our local super market, from Amazon, or borrowed from our families.

Section 7: Financial Plan

Cashflow Forecast

TIME	WEEK 1	WEEK 2	WEEK 3	WEEK 4	TOTAL
Number of cookies sold ($1.50)	0	40	52	65	157
Number of brownies sold ($2.00)	0	12	24	33	69

	WEEK 1	WEEK 2	WEEK 3	WEEK 4	TOTAL
Income					
Investor Income	$80.00	$0.00	$0.00	$0.00	$80.00
Sales Income	$0	$84.00	$126.00	$163.50	$373.50
A) Total Income	$80.00	$84.00	$126.00	$163.50	$453.50

	WEEK 1	WEEK 2	WEEK 3	WEEK 4	TOTAL
Expenditure					
Mixing Bowls	$13.00				$13.00
Cookie Sheets	$14.00				$14.00
Baking Tins	$8.00		$8.00		$16.00
Flour	$7.76				$7.76
Chocolate Chips	$7.30		$7.30		$14.60
Sugar	$6.36			$6.36	$12.72
Eggs	$1.97		$1.97		$3.94
Cacao Powder	$5.99				$5.99
Baking Powder	$4.99				$4.99
Vanilla Extract	$7.36				$7.36
Butter	$2.96		$2.96	$2.96	$8.88
Employee Wage	$0				
Investor Pay	$0	$40	$40		$80
Uniforms	$0			$36.00	$36.00
Sales Booth				$50.00	$50.00
Website				$20.00	$20.00
B) Total Expenditure	$79.69	$40	$60.23	$115.32	$295.24

C) Income – Expenditure (A–B)	$0.31	$44.00	$65.77	$48.18	$158.26
Opening Balance (previous week closing balance)	$0	$0.31	$44.31	$110.08	$0
Closing Balance	$0.31	$44.31	$110.08	$158.26	$158.26

Cash Flow Statement

Date	Description	Income	Expense	Balance
Jan 10th	Owner Input from Alan, Mary, Doug	$80		$80
Jan 14th	Supplies: Ingredients		$44.69	$35.31
Jan 15th	Supplies: Baking tins, cookie sheet, mixing bowl		$35	$0.31
Jan 17th	Sales : 20 cookies, 12 brownies	$54		$54.31
Jan 19th	Sales: 18 cookies, 12 brownies	$51		$105.31
Jan 21st	Return investor money Part 1		$40	$65.31
Jan 24th	Sales: 24 cookies, 16 brownies	$68		$133.31
Jan 26th	Sales: 32 cookies, 24 brownies	$96		$229.31
Jan 28th	Return Investor Money Part		$40	$189.31
Jan 30th	Supplies: Ingredients		$88.38	$10.93
Feb 1st	Sales: 26 cookies, 20 brownies	$79		$179.93
Feb 3rd	Sales: 40 cookies, 24 brownies	$108		$287.93

Cashflow Statement for: January 5th–February 3rd	
Opening Balance	$0
Income from sales	$456
Income from other sources	$80
Operating expenses	–$168.07
Repayment of loans/investors	–$80
Closing Balance	$287.93
Profit/Loss (Closing Balance – Opening Balance)	$287.93

APPENDIX 5: SAMPLE BUSINESS PLAN

Balance Sheet

Balance Sheet: up to February 5th			
Assets			
	Cash/Account Balance	$287.93	
	Equipment	$36	Estimated resale value of: Bowls, cookie sheets, baking tin, mixer
	Materials	$10	Leftover ingredients
	Unsold Product Value	$0	Gave away before they expired
	Money Owed	$0	All cookies and brownies were paid for
Liabilities			
	Unpaid Bills	$0	
	Money Owed for loans/investors	$0	All investors have been paid back
Balance (Assets - Liabilities)		$333.93	$111.31 per partner if we stop now

Section 8: Appendices and Exhibits

Chocolate Chip Cookie Recipe

Ingredients

- 1 cup salted butter
- 1 cup white (granulated) sugar
- 1 cup light brown sugar packed
- 2 tsp pure vanilla extract
- 2 large eggs
- 3 cups all-purpose flour
- 1 tsp baking soda
- ½ tsp baking powder
- 1 tsp sea salt
- 2 cups chocolate chips (or chunks, or chopped chocolate)

Instructions

1. Preheat oven to 375 degrees F. Line a baking pan with parchment paper and set aside.
2. In a separate bowl mix flour, baking soda, salt, baking powder. Set aside.
3. Cream together butter and sugars until combined.
4. Beat in eggs and vanilla until fluffy.
5. Mix in the dry ingredients until combined.

6. Add 12 oz package of chocolate chips and mix well.
7. Roll 2 tbsp of dough at a time into balls and place them evenly spaced on your prepared cookie sheets.
8. Bake in preheated oven for approximately 8-10 minutes. Take them out when the edges start to turn brown.
9. Let them sit on the baking pan for 2 minutes before transferring to cooling rack.

Nutrition

- Serving: 1 cookie
- Calories: 263.4kcal | Carbohydrates: 41.2g| Protein: 2.7g | Fat: 12.6g | Cholesterol: 31.6mg | Potassium: 115.4mg | Fiber: 1.4g | Sugar: 25.5g | Vitamin A: 5.2% | Calcium: 2.3% | Iron: 7%

Brownie Recipe

Ingredients

- 1/2 cup + 2 tablespoons salted butter melted
- 1 cup granulated sugar
- 2 large eggs
- 2 teaspoons vanilla extract
- 1/2 cup melted milk chocolate chips
- 3/4 cup all-purpose flour
- 1/4 cup unsweetened cocoa powder
- 1/2 teaspoon salt
- 1 cup milk chocolate chips

Instructions

1. Preheat oven to 350 degrees F. Line a metal 9x9 pan with parchment paper.
2. Pour melted butter into a large mixing bowl. Whisk in sugar by hand until smooth, 30 seconds.
3. Add in eggs and vanilla extract. Whisk 1 minute.
4. Whisk in melted chocolate until combined and smooth.
5. Use a rubber spatula to stir in flour, cocoa powder, and salt until just combined. Stir in whole chocolate chips.
6. Pour into prepared pan and smooth out.
7. Bake in the preheated oven for 30 minutes. Let cool in pan 30 minutes before slicing.

Nutrition

- Serving: 1 brownie
- Calories: 386kcal | Carbohydrates: 52g | Protein: 4g | Fat: 18g | Saturated Fat : 11g | Cholesterol: 67mg | Sodium: 254mg | Potassium: 61mg | Fiber: 1g | Sugar: 41g | Vitamin A: 8.7% | Vitamin C: 0.1% | Calcium: 4.8% | Iron: 7.5%

APPENDIX 6
RESOURCES

Websites and Tools Mentioned in this Workbook

Canva
Used for creating original graphics that can be used in your marketing material, such as your logo design.
www.canva.com

Fiverr
Fiverr is a freelance site in which people sell their digital skills such as graphic design, website building, marketing campaigns, social media management, and a ton more. You can hire people from anywhere as low as $5.
www.fiverr.com

Wix
Website building tool with free options and relatively easy to use for a beginner.
www.wix.com

Weebly
Another website building tool with free options.
www.weebly.com

Google Sites
A common website building tool for schools and very easy to get started with.
sites.google.com

Word Press
Regarded as one of the best website building tools available for beginners. You can build directly on their site, or you can often use their web building tool when hosting your site somewhere else. There are lots of instructional videos available on how to do this.
www.wordpress.com

Recommended Blogs, Books, Podcasts, and Video Channels Regarding Entrepreneurship

Blogs and Podcasts
- ChooseFI
- Smart Passive Income
- Making Sense of Cents
- Afford Anything
- The FI Show
- Side Hustle Nation

Books
- 4-Hour Work Week—Tim Ferris
- The Lean Startup—Eric Reis
- The $100 Startup—Chris Gullebeau
- Rich Dad, Poor Dad—Robert Kiyosaki
- Founders at Work: Stories of Startups' Early Days—Jessica Livingston
- The Seven Habits of Highly Effective People—Stephen Covey
- Small Business Finance for the Busy Entrepreneur: Blueprint for Building a Solid, Profitable Business—Sylvia Inks

APPENDIX 7
GLOSSARY

A

Advertise - describe or draw attention to a product, service, or event in a public medium in order to promote sales or attendance.

Advertisement - a notice or announcement in a public medium promoting a product, service, or event or publicizing a job vacancy.

Advertising Campaign - an organized course of action to promote a product or service.

Angel Investor - a wealthy person who invests their own money in a company, usually in the early stages of development.

Asset - parts of the business with a positive value.

Autonomy - freedom to make your own choices.

B

Balance Sheet - summarizes a company's assets, liabilities, and owners' equity at a specific point in time.

Blog - a website with an informational focus, run by small groups or individuals, written in an informal or conversational style.

Brainstorm - a process for producing ideas or solving problems.

Brand - the marketing practice of creating a name, symbol, or design that identifies and differentiates a product from other products.

Brand Loyalty - the tendency of customers to buy one brand over competing brands.

Break-Even Analysis - the process of determining the level of sales needed to cover the costs of a business.

Break-Even Point - the unit number of sales needed to match the costs of a business.

Break-Even Pricing - setting the price of a product or service to simply meet the costs needed to produce it.

Budget - an estimation of planned income and expenses over a period of time.

Bulk Purchase - purchasing a product or service in large quantities.

Bundling - the grouping of products or services into a single sale or contract.

Business Plan - a written document describing the nature of the business, the sales and marketing strategy, and the financial background, and containing a projected profit and loss statement.

C

Capital - finances needed by a business to produce goods or provide services.

Cashflow - measures how much cash a company takes in versus how much it expends.

Cashflow Statement - a recording of the income and expenses of a business in a past time period.

Cashflow Forecast - a prediction of expected income and expenses for a business in a given period.

Certified Public Accountant (CPA) - a professional who helps an individual or business with the maintenance of their financial records and payment of taxes.

Chief Executive Officer (CEO) - the highest-ranking person in a company who is responsible for all major decision making and team management.

Chief Financial Officer (CFO) - responsible for managing the finances of a business.

Cold-Call - the process of reaching out to people that you have no prior connection with.

Competitive Analysis - an investigation into the strengths and weaknesses of a competing business to your own.

Competitive Pricing - setting your price to be around the same as your competitors.

Competitor – an individual or a business which you are directly competing against for a customer's business.

Consumer – a user of a product or service from a business.

Contract – a formal and binding agreement with the duties, roles, and expectations of all concerned parties listed.

Contractor – an individual or company that agrees to a contract to perform a task for a business.

Cost-Plus Pricing – setting a price to be the cost of producing it plus a given amount or percentage.

Crowdfund – gathering small amounts of money from a large number of people to fund a large project.

Customer – a person or business that buys products and services.

Customer Service – the assistance and advice provided by a business to its customers.

D

Debt – when you owe money to someone else.

Delegate – entrust someone else with the responsibility for a task.

Demographic – the characteristics of a population.

Digital Payment – any form of payment that is made using a digital platform. No physical currency is used.

Domain Name – your website name.

E

Economy – the wealth and resources of an area.

Efficient – increased productivity with reduced effort.

Elevator Pitch – a short, prepared speech that explains who you are and what your business does in a clear and succinct way.

Employee – a person working for wages or a salary in a business.

Endorsement – give your public recommendation of a person, business, product, or service.

Entrepreneur – a person who owns, operates, and organizes a business while assuming all financial risk and reward.

Entrepreneurship – the action of setting up a business while assuming all risk and reward.

Environmental, Social, Governance (ESG) – these are criteria used to evaluate a business regarding its sustainability.

Exchange of Services – a trade where each side performs a service for the other instead of using currency.

F

F.O.M.O. – short for fear of missing out. Refers to a person's likelihood to act if they fear there is limited opportunity to do so.

Fad – a high interest in something by a large number of people, but which is very short-lived.

Fair Trade – all contributors to the final product were paid a fair price for the materials or service.

Feedback – the reactions to a product or service. Can include likes, dislikes, ideas, concerns.

Finance – the funds needed to complete a project.

Financial Projection – the predicted cashflow of a business including revenue and expenses.

Fixed Costs – the costs of a business that are still there even if nothing is produced.

Focus Group – a small group that represents a sample of the market, who give their opinions to pre-determined discussion questions.

Freelance – to sell one's skills to a variety of businesses without being tied to one of them.

H

Hashtag – a word or phrase with a # in front of it, used to group content with a similar theme or topic together.

Hobby – an activity done regularly in one's leisure time for pleasure.

Hospitality Industry - an industry concerned with providing services to customers.

Household Income - the total income of all residents of a household.

Human Resources - part of a business that deals with the hiring, firing, administration, and training of staff.

I

Industry - a section of all business with distinct characteristics.

Influencer - a person or business who can affect the opinions of others due to their popularity, perceived knowledge, or title.

Internal Revenue Service (IRS) - a branch of the US government that oversees the collection of taxes.

Inventory - the materials, completed goods, and equipment owned by a business at a given point in time.

Investor - someone who purchases ownership or loans money with the expectation of increasing the value of their money over time.

J

Job Description - a written account of the roles and responsibilities of an individual within a business.

L

Lease - a rental agreement in which you pay to use a property or an item, but you do not own it.

Liability - parts of the business which have a negative value or where money is owed.

Limited Liability Company (LLC) – a business structure in which the owner is legally separate from the business. The owners are not personally liable for the debts of the business.

Living Document - a document which is continually being updated and edited.

Logo - the symbol for a business.

Loss - the revenue of a business, product, or service does not exceed the costs of running or producing it.

Loss Leader - setting the price of an item to be lower than all competitors in order to attract customers to your business.

M

Management - a position of having to be responsible for another person's actions and tasks.

Manufacturer - a business that produces a product from raw materials.

Margin of Safety - the amount the sales of a business can fall before turning into a loss.

Market - the group of people who could potentially buy from a business.

Market Research - the gathering of information about the market including needs, wants, and preferences.

Market Segmentation - dividing the market based on certain characteristics.

Market Share - the percentage of your target market which buys from you.

Marketing - the act of how you set up your business to meet the needs of your target market, and how you make your business as appealing as possible to that market in efforts to get them to buy from you.

Marketing Mix - a plan detailing the Product, Price, Promotion, Place, and Packaging for your business.

Media - a method of mass communication with people.

Mission - a written statement of how a business plans to serve its target market and its goals.

Monopoly - the only provider of a good or service in an area. A lack of competition.

Mortgage - a type of loan given for purchases of property.

N

Need - something which you cannot live without.

APPENDIX 7: GLOSSARY

Net Worth - the value of what an individual owns minus what they owe (Assets - Liabilities = Net Worth).

Network - the collection of people that you know.

Networking - the act of increasing your network.

Niche Market - a small segment of the market with a very specific focus.

Non-Profit - a business which does not exist to be profitable.

O

Observation - watching and recording behaviors, without influencing them, to gather information.

Operating Plan - outlines the physical requirements of your business, such as a sales table, storage, retail space, equipment, inventory and supplies, labor, etc.

Opportunities - things outside of your control that are positive for you or your business.

Organic Growth - increasing the size of a business using the profits already generated. No extra capital is used.

Outsource - hire someone external to the business to perform a task for the business.

P

Partnership - a simple business model consisting of two or more people who agree to share responsibility for a business.

Penetration Pricing - setting your price low initially to gain a customer following and then increasing prices gradually.

Point of Sale - where the customer can make a purchase from a business.

Price - the amount charged for a product or service.

Price Discrimination - special pricing for different segments of the market.

Price Leadership - setting your price higher than the competition to give the impression of superior value.

Pricing Strategy - the method used for determining the price of a product or service.

Primary Research - new research which involves gathering new data that has not been collected before.

Produce - to make.

Product - a physical item sold by a business.

Product Placement – when businesses pay for their products to be used in media such as TV or movies.

Profit - a financial gain, especially the difference between the amount earned and the amount spent in buying, operating, or producing something.

Profitable - has positive value when sales revenue is compared with costs.

Promote - to support.

Prototype - a working model of your product.

Q

Qualitative Data - measures of 'types' and may be represented by a name, symbol, or a number code.

Quality Control - the system put in place to make sure all products and services meet the minimum required standards of a business.

Quantitative Data - measures of values or counts and are expressed as numbers.

R

Recurring Costs - costs which occur at regular increments.

Responsibility - having accountability for an action or task being completed. Assuming all blame for consequences.

Revenue - the income of a business.

Risk - the probability of failure or loss.

S

Sales - the number of units sold or the currency value of the units sold.

Scarcity Mindset - a fear that something will run out or there is not enough of it.

Secondary Research - research that involves gathering existing data that has already been produced.

Service - a skill that is performed and sold by a business.

Social Media - websites, applications, and other platforms that enable us to share or create content and participate in social networks that mimic in person networks.

Social Network - the extent of the personal relationships of an individual.

Sole Proprietor - a business with a single owner that has no legal separation from the owner.

Staffing - the workers needed by a business to allow it to operate.

Standard - a level of quality.

Strengths - things that you or your business do well.

Subcontract - hire someone outside of the business to complete a task.

Survey - a set of questions in which respondents provide their opinions, feelings, thoughts. Surveys can be written, interview based, or digital.

Sustainable - deemed to not deplete natural resources and promotes equality in the workforce.

T

Target Market - the portion of the market that is most likely to buy your product or service.

Telecommunications - the exchange of information by electronic means.

Threats - factors external to a person or business which are negative.

Total Costs - the sum of the fixed costs and variable costs of a business.

Trend - a changing behavior common to a large group of people.

Twitter Handle - the username on a Twitter account which is also used to reference or "tag" an account in a post.

U

Unique Selling Point (USP) - a feature of a product or service which sets it apart from its competition in an appealing way to customers.

URL - the address of a website page. Starts with www.

Utilities - the collection of services including electric, gas, water, and sewage.

V

Valuation - the determined value of an item or service.

Values - what an individual or organization considers to be of importance.

Variable Costs - the costs that increase or decrease with the level of production.

Venture Capitalist - a individual or company that invests a pool of smaller investor's money into start-up companies with high growth potential in exchange for part ownership.

Viable - capable of working successfully.

W

Wants - things that you can live without, but you desire to have.

Weaknesses - things that you or your business do not currently do well.

Website - a location on the internet where information can be displayed.

Y

Y.O.L.O. - short for you only live once. A justification for making a decision due to not knowing what could happen tomorrow.

APPENDIX 8
BIBLIOGRAPHY

All Business Editors (2019) *The Five Basic Methods of Market Research*, [online] available at: https://www.allbusiness.com/the-five-basic-methods-of-market-research-1287-1.html, Accessed: 7/14/19

Boyer, H. (2017) *Creating a Pattern is a lot like Building an App: The Product Design Process*, [online] available at: http://hboyer.com/product-design-process, Accessed 4/12/19

Controller, C. (2018) *How to Calculate Manufacturing Costs Per Unit*, [online] available at: https://www.completecontroller.com/how-to-calculate-manufacturing-cost-per-unit, Accessed: 7/14/19

Donegan, A. (2018) *Pop-up Business School*, [online] available at: https://www.popupbusinessschool.co.uk, Accessed 1/15/19

Doyle, A (2019) *Important Business Skills for Workplace Success*, [online] available at: https://www.thebalancecareers.com/business-skills-list-2062366, Accessed: 6/3/19

Gillespie, J. (2016) *What is Cash Flow Forecasting?* [online] available at: https://www.cashanalytics.com/what-is-cash-flow-forecasting, Accessed 7/14/19

Hanlon, A. (2013) *Examples and Tips for Using AIDA in the Real World*, [online] available at: https://www.smartinsights.com/traffic-building-strategy/offer-and-message-development/aida-model, Accessed: 5/22/19

Johnson, J. (2017) *Elements of a Business Plan*, Entreprenuer.com, [online] available at: https://www.entrepreneur.com/article/38308, Accessed 2/5/19

Katen, L. (2019) *Perfect Pitch: How to Nail Your Elevator Speech*, [online] available at: https://www.themuse.com/advice/perfect-pitch-how-to-nail-your-elevator-speech, Accessed 6/10/19

Mind Tools (2018) *SWOT Analysis: Discover New Opportunities, Manage and Eliminate Threats*, [online] available at: https://www.mindtools.com/pages/article/newTMC_05.htm, Accessed 1/15/19

Osterwalder, A. (2005) *Business Model Canvas* [online] available at: https://www.strategyzer.com/canvas, Accessed: 5/6/19

Ries, E. (2011). *The Lean Startup: How today's entrepreneurs use continuous innovation to create radically successful businesses*. New York: Crown Business.

Riley, J. (2018) *Tutor2U*, [online] available at: https://www.tutor2u.net/business/reference/organisation-charts, Accessed 7/14/19

Ryan, A. (2003) *Student Enterprise Awards Workbook*, Ireland: County & City Enterprise Boards

About the Author

Rob Phelan is an entrepreneur and high school personal finance teacher in Maryland. He is a Certified Financial Education Instructor by NCFE and has also co-created the ChooseFI K-12 Financial Education Curriculum. Rob has helped his students form over 60 student businesses, some of which have won recognition at entrepreneurship competitions in Maryland.

For more information and ongoing support for your Simple StartUp, visit www.thesimplestartup.com

www.ingramcontent.com/pod-product-compliance
Lightning Source LLC
Chambersburg PA
CBHW061119010526
44112CB00024B/2913